MW01165098

Program Guide

Surviving & Thriving
IN THE CLASSROOM

GRADES 6-8

Printed in the U.S.A.

ISBN 978-0-358-43694-2

2 3 4 5 6 7 8 9 10   0607   29 28 27 26 25 24 23 22 21

4500824514

r10.20

Connected Teaching for ELA Educators

Dear Educators,

At HMH, **we have been listening** to your needs. Lean on us to help you

- connect students to the right **instruction**
- deliver flexible and innovative learning experiences built on the foundations of **best teaching practices** and **educational research**
- **bridge the digital divide** with instruction available in both print and digital formats, accessible online and offline
- provide a **reliable and valid growth measure** that monitors progress and achievement
- implement traditional classroom teaching and the tools to deliver instruction through **remote learning**
- foster students' **social and emotional growth** and build resilience through embedded SEL support
- teach with continuous, connected **professional learning** . . . and *do what you do best*

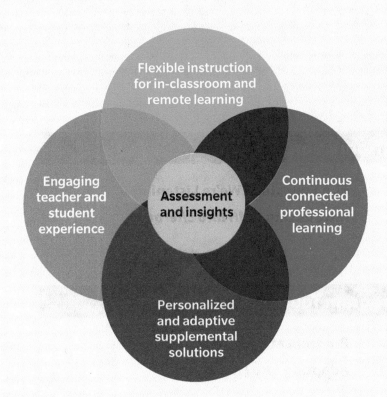

Flexible instruction for in-classroom and remote learning

Engaging teacher and student experience

Assessment and insights

Continuous connected professional learning

Personalized and adaptive supplemental solutions

Take a Look!

This Program Guide is your **professional companion** to help you to learn about your new program, *HMH Into Literature*.

Let's go!

Table of Contents

Meeting the Needs of ELA Educators

ELA Educators, We're Listening

HMH Into Literature was inspired by you—your words, your instructional needs, your pain points, your questions. Here are some of the common threads affecting ELA educators today.

Flexibility & Choice

WHAT WE HEARD

"Curriculum and texts are standardized at the district level. Where do I have flexibility and choice?"

"I want to incorporate novels and longer reads into my instruction."

"It's too hard to figure out how any new program can meet my specific needs."

WHAT WE DID

1. ✓ Developed flexible unit and lesson planning resources, built with realistic pacing in mind

2. ✓ Helped you integrate novels, differentiate instruction, and use additional texts for whole-class and independent reading

3. ✓ Made it easier for you to use only those resources or instructional aspects that work for you

Engagement & Cultural Relevance

WHAT WE HEARD

"Students need to see themselves in what they read."

"It's hard work to engage students and get them to want to read."

"I know the classics; I need more contemporary, diverse connections."

WHAT WE DID

1. ✓ Curated high-interest units of culturally relevant and diverse texts that middle-schoolers will want to read and discuss

2. ✓ Included activities to engage and motivate students and appeal to their varied interests

Student Growth & Outcomes
WHAT WE HEARD

"How students do on standardized testing affects everything for me."

"I need to know the best way to cover my state's standards."

WHAT WE DID

1. ☑ Ensured that you can cover all of your state's standards and gave you a road map for doing so

2. ☑ Gave you embedded and frequent practice in the formats of your state's summative test

3. ☑ Made sure that you have multiple ways to assess students' understanding and mastery of the standards

Lack of Time & Support
WHAT WE HEARD

"I'm new to the profession. Help!"

"Teacher burnout is real. It's never been harder to be a classroom teacher."

"There is simply not enough time to support all the student needs in my classes."

WHAT WE DID

1. ☑ Offered you the same scaffolding, tips, and strategies that we give to students; from first-year teachers to veterans, we want you to feel that "you've got this"

2. ☑ Gave you frequent insights into how your students are doing and recommended resources that can help them, no matter the need

3. ☑ Saved you time through data insights and resource suggestions

Writing

WHAT WE HEARD

"How do I effectively teach my students how to write?"

"I don't have time to grade what students write!"

"Students need more practice with the kinds of writing they encounter on high-stakes assessments."

WHAT WE DID

1. ✓ Provided more writing activities, prompts, and support—including both creative writing and writing modeled after summative assessments

2. ✓ Gave you access to Writable with digital tools, such as Turn It In, peer review, and Revision Aid, to ease some of the burden on you when grading student work

3. ✓ Tried to demystify teaching writing, so that you have the support you need to guide your students

Integrated Social & Emotional Learning

WHAT WE HEARD

"There is a big push for social-emotional learning in my district. How do I work it in?"

"We have a polarized culture. How do I navigate classroom conversations about difficult topics and texts?"

WHAT WE DID

1. ✓ Included more provocative texts worth debating—and gave you support for facilitating respectful discussions in class

2. ✓ Connected social and emotional learning activities and instruction into each lesson

Effective Use of Technology

WHAT WE HEARD

"My school has a learning management system. Show me how your resources can plug into what I am already using."

"I need to make sure any technology I use is reliable and user-friendly—whether I am teaching in the classroom or remotely."

"I need more support for meaningful integration of technology."

WHAT WE DID

1. ☑ Made all core content available online and offline (through our offline app), providing you with the flexibility to teach in the classroom or remotely

2. ☑ Gave tips, support, and ideas for implementing a blended-learning classroom and teaching remotely

3. ☑ Built in point-of-use tips and recommendations for incorporating digital resources

4. ☑ Provided all texts in printable format and assessments in editable format, giving you more flexibility for offline usage

5. ☑ Made it easier for you to integrate with other systems and tools, like Google Classroom

Connecting Your Expertise and *Into Literature* . . .

We've got this.

Introducing
HMH Into Literature

Connected Teaching

HMH Into Literature offers rich content, actionable insights, personalized learning, and standards-based instruction—**all within one seamless experience**. With HMH's system of connected solutions, you and your students have access to

- assessments that pinpoint learning gaps, as well as driving content and grouping recommendations
- instruction that provides the flexibility for whole-class, small-group, and independent, personalized learning
- professional learning that is embedded within the instruction and available to enrich and enhance the classroom experience

HMH Into Literature provides the instructional tools, rich pedagogy, and professional services to ensure that you and your students not only reach—but exceed—your instructional goals.

Rich Content and Standards-Based Instruction

- Research-based, explicit, and systematic instruction
- Resources and support for whole-class, small-group, and independent work
- Materials for striving readers and writers, English learners, and advanced learners

Assessments and Actionable Insights

- Embedded formative and summative assessments
- Growth Measure reports that help inform instructional decisions, planning, and grouping

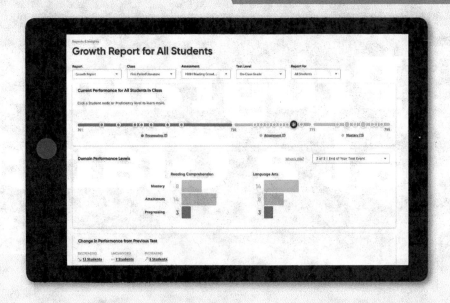

Professional Learning

- **Getting Started** for every teacher
- Curated, on-demand, curriculum-aligned content through **Teacher's Corner**
- Online team coaching tailored to your learning needs

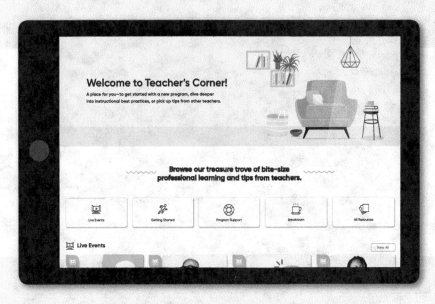

Supplemental Digital Practice and Instruction

- Personalized reading practice to address skills diversity
- Writing practice and feedback with customizable assignments that support *HMH Into Literature*

Writable

Waggle

Program at a Glance

Overview

Here is everything you need to make *HMH Into Literature* work in your classroom.

In each grade, a consumable **Student Edition** provides high-interest units and text sets. Wrapped around those texts are instruction and practice in key skills. **Notice & Note** protocol for close reading is also integrated into each lesson.

A **Teacher's Edition** provides point-of-use instructional support and differentiation. It outlines how you can make each unit and lesson your own, using the resources in a way that works best for your classroom.

Ed: Your Friend in Learning provides resources and functionality for flexible teaching and meaningful, interactive learning. Find:

- student eBooks with audio, video, annotation, and note-taking functions
- assessments and practice that mirror high-stakes assessment formats
- lesson-planning tools
- data insights on student growth and proficiency, along with recommendations

This **Program Guide** is your starting point for learning about the program—its research base, instructional design, components, and flexible options for implementation.

Novels and Long Reads recommendations accompany each unit. Consult these recommendations to help you decide which titles to include in your package.

Unit at a Glance

Each unit follows a consistent instructional design, grounded in a gradual-release model that moves students from whole-class learning to peer collaboration to independence.

1 Each unit in *Into Literature* focuses on a **high-interest topic** and **Essential Question**, which students explore through different genres.

2 **Spark Your Learning** features activities and prompts for engaging students and building their topic knowledge.

6 Each unit includes one or two **Mentor Texts**, authentic examples of the writing students will be asked to do in the cumulative task.

UNIT
1

Reality Check
Page 1

? **1** ESSENTIAL QUESTION:
What can blur the lines between what's real and what's not?

KEY LEARNING OBJECTIVES
- Analyze plot
- Analyze character traits
- Analyze folktales
- Analyze rhyme and rhyme scheme
- Analyze sound devices and mood
- Analyze narrator
- Evaluate graphic novel

Units are divided into three sections:

3 **Analyze & Apply** —perfect for whole-class learning

4 **Collaborate & Compare** —for peer and small-group work

5 **Reader's Choice** —short and long reads for independent reading

UNIT **1**

7 **End-of-unit tasks** in writing and speaking and listening allow students to demonstrate their understanding of learning objectives and offer new insights into the Essential Question.

Writable

All writing prompts, including unit tasks, are available to assign within **Writable**.

Ed

Go online for

Unit and Selection Videos

Interactive Annotation and Text Analysis

Selection Audio Recordings

Collaborative Writing **Writable**

Lesson at a Glance

Each lesson also follows a consistent structure, with activities and instruction occurring before, during, and after reading. Take a closer look at each section on the following pages.

Get Ready

Each lesson opens with a **Get Ready** feature, which provides activities, background, and instruction that prepare students for reading.

Instructional Features:

1 Engage Your Brain

2 Skills-Based Instruction

3 Annotation in Action

4 Expand Your Vocabulary

5 Background

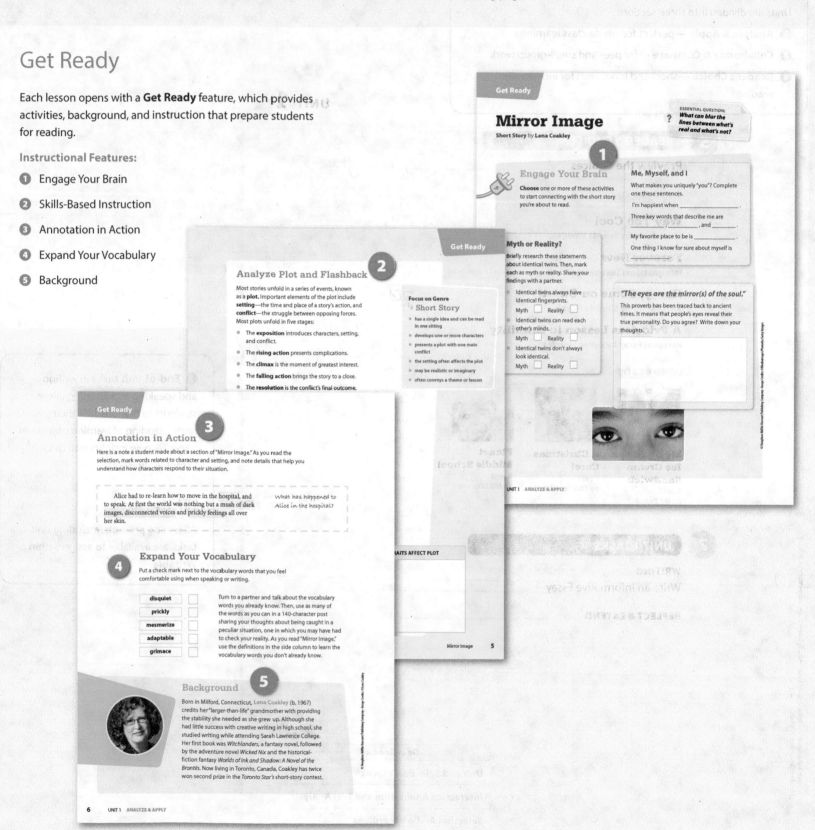

Get Ready

Mirror Image

Short Story by Lena Coakley

ESSENTIAL QUESTION:
What can blur the lines between what's real and what's not?

1

Engage Your Brain

Choose one or more of these activities to start connecting with the short story you're about to read.

Me, Myself, and I

What makes you uniquely "you"? Complete one these sentences.

I'm happiest when _____ .

Three key words that describe me are _____ , and _____ .

My favorite place to be is _____ .

One thing I know for sure about myself is _____

Myth or Reality?

Briefly research these statements about identical twins. Then, mark each as myth or reality. Share your findings with a partner.

- Identical twins always have identical fingerprints.
  Myth ☐ Reality ☐
- Identical twins can read each other's minds.
  Myth ☐ Reality ☐
- Identical twins don't always look identical.
  Myth ☐ Reality ☐

"The eyes are the mirror(s) of the soul."

This proverb has been traced back to ancient times. It means that people's eyes reveal their true personality. Do you agree? Write down your thoughts.

UNIT 1 ANALYZE & APPLY

Get Ready

Analyze Plot and Flashback

2

Most stories unfold in a series of events, known as a **plot**. Important elements of the plot include **setting**—the time and place of a story's action, and **conflict**—the struggle between opposing forces. Most plots unfold in five stages:

- The **exposition** introduces characters, setting, and conflict.
- The **rising action** presents complications.
- The **climax** is the moment of greatest interest.
- The **falling action** brings the story to a close.
- The **resolution** is the conflict's final outcome.

Focus on Genre

↪ Short Story

- has a single idea and can be read in one sitting
- develops one or more characters
- presents a plot with one main conflict
- the setting often affects the plot
- may be realistic or imaginary
- often conveys a theme or lesson

Get Ready

Annotation in Action

3

Here is a note a student made about a section of "Mirror Image." As you read the selection, mark words related to character and setting, and note details that help you understand how characters respond to their situation.

> Alice had to re-learn how to move in the hospital, and to speak. At first the world was nothing but a mush of dark images, disconnected voices and prickly feelings all over her skin.

What has happened to Alice in the hospital?

Expand Your Vocabulary

4

Put a check mark next to the vocabulary words that you feel comfortable using when speaking or writing.

disquiet	☐
prickly	☐
mesmerize	☐
adaptable	☐
grimace	☐

Turn to a partner and talk about the vocabulary words you already know. Then, use as many of the words as you can in a 140-character post sharing your thoughts about being caught in a peculiar situation, one in which you may have had to check your reality. As you read "Mirror Image," use the definitions in the side column to learn the vocabulary words you don't already know.

Mirror Image 5

Background

5

Born in Milford, Connecticut, Lena Coakley (b. 1967) credits her "larger-than-life" grandmother with providing the stability she needed as she grew up. Although she had little success with creative writing in high school, she studied writing while attending Sarah Lawrence College. Her first book was *Witchlanders*, a fantasy novel, followed by the adventure novel *Wicked Nix* and the historical-fiction fantasy *Worlds of Ink and Shadow: A Novel of the Brontës*. Now living in Toronto, Canada, Coakley has twice won second prize in the *Toronto Star*'s short-story contest.

6 UNIT 1 ANALYZE & APPLY

Read

As students read, they are prompted to annotate and analyze the text carefully.

Instructional Features:

- **6** Standards-Based Guided Reading Questions with Annotation
- **7** Notice & Note Signposts
- **8** Vocabulary in Context
- **9** Assessment Practice

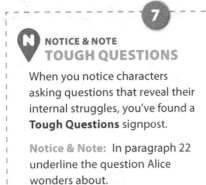

7

N NOTICE & NOTE
TOUGH QUESTIONS

When you notice characters asking questions that reveal their internal struggles, you've found a **Tough Questions** signpost.

Notice & Note: In paragraph 22 underline the question Alice wonders about.

Analyze question about?

ANALYZE CHARACTER TRAITS

Annotate: Review Jenny's description of Alice in paragraph 65. Mark any details that show Alice's current traits.

6

Analyze: What does Jenny's description reveal about her relationship with Alice at this point?

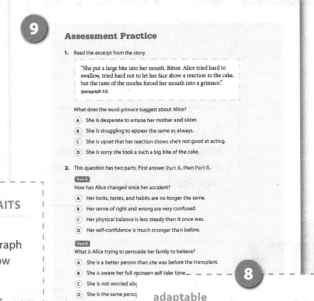

9

Assessment Practice

1. Read the excerpt from the story.

> "She put a large bite into her mouth. Bitter. Alice tried hard to swallow, tried hard not to let her face show a reaction to the cake, but the taste of the mocha forced her mouth into a grimace."
> (paragraph 53)

What does the word *grimace* suggest about Alice?

- A She is desperate to amuse her mother and sister.
- B She is struggling to appear the same as always.
- C She is upset that her reaction shows she's not good at acting.
- D She is sorry she took a such a big bite of the cake.

2. This question has two parts. First answer Part A, then Part B.

Part A
How has Alice changed since her accident?

- A Her looks, tastes, and habits are no longer the same.
- B Her sense of right and wrong are very confused.
- C Her physical balance is less steady than it once was.
- D Her self-confidence is much stronger than before.

Part B
What is Alice trying to persuade her family to believe?

- A She is a better person than she was before the transplant.
- B She is aware her full recovery will take time.
- C She is not worried ab...
- D She is the same pers...

8

adaptable
(ə-dăp´tə-bəl) *adj.* Something that is *adaptable* can change or adjust to meet new conditions.

Mirror Image **15**

Respond

After reading, students respond to the text in a variety of ways.

Instructional Features:

- **10** Analyze the Text Questions
- **11** Choices
- **12** Expand Your Vocabulary
- **13** Watch Your Language!

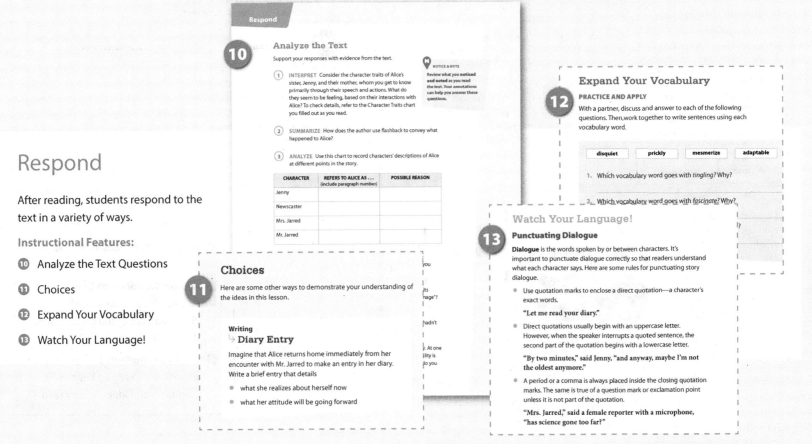

Respond

Analyze the Text

Support your responses with evidence from the text.

10

1 **INTERPRET** Consider the character traits of Alice's sister, Jenny, and their mother, whom you get to know primarily through their speech and actions. What do they seem to be feeling, based on their interactions with Alice? To check details, refer to the Character Traits chart you filled out as you read.

2 **SUMMARIZE** How does the author use flashback to convey what happened to Alice?

3 **ANALYZE** Use this chart to record characters' descriptions of Alice at different points in the story.

N NOTICE & NOTE
Review what you **noticed and noted** as you read the text. Your annotations can help you answer these questions.

CHARACTER	REFERS TO ALICE AS ... (include paragraph number)	POSSIBLE REASON
Jenny		
Newscaster		
Mrs. Jarred		
Mr. Jarred		

11

Choices

Here are some other ways to demonstrate your understanding of the ideas in this lesson.

Writing
↳ **Diary Entry**

Imagine that Alice returns home immediately from her encounter with Mr. Jarred to make an entry in her diary. Write a brief entry that details

- what she realizes about herself now
- what her attitude will be going forward

12

Expand Your Vocabulary

PRACTICE AND APPLY

With a partner, discuss and answer to each of the following questions. Then, work together to write sentences using each vocabulary word.

disquiet	prickly	mesmerize	adaptable

1. Which vocabulary word goes with *tingling*? Why?

2. Which vocabulary word goes with *fascinate*? Why?

Watch Your Language!

13

Punctuating Dialogue

Dialogue is the words spoken by or between characters. It's important to punctuate dialogue correctly so that readers understand what each character says. Here are some rules for punctuating story dialogue.

- Use quotation marks to enclose a direct quotation—a character's exact words.

  "Let me read your diary."

- Direct quotations usually begin with an uppercase letter. However, when the speaker interrupts a quoted sentence, the second part of the quotation begins with a lowercase letter.

  "By two minutes," said Jenny, **"and anyway, maybe I'm not the oldest anymore."**

- A period or a comma is always placed inside the closing quotation marks. The same is true of a question mark or exclamation point unless it is not part of the quotation.

  "Mrs. Jarred," said a female reporter with a microphone, **"has science gone too far?"**

Teaching a Lesson: Get Ready

❶ Use the quick **Engage Your Brain** activities to motivate your students and get them talking and writing about key ideas related to each text.

Analyze Plot and Flashback ❷

Most stories unfold in a series of events, known as a **plot**. Important elements of the plot include **setting**—the time and place of a story's action, and **conflict**—the struggle between opposing forces. Most plots unfold in five stages:

- The **exposition** introduces characters, setting, and conflict.
- The **rising action** presents complications.
- The **climax** is the moment of greatest interest.
- The **falling action** brings the story to a close.
- The **resolution** is the conflict's final outcome.

Some plots include a device called a **flashback** that can interrupt a story's chronological order by describing what took place at an earlier time. The details of flashbacks help readers better understand the story's current plot developments.

Analyze Character Traits

The **characters** in a short story are the people, animals, or imaginary creatures that take part in the action. Characters have personal qualities known as **character traits.** An author often describes characters' qualities and appearance directly, but just as often, a reader must figure out characters' traits based on their actions and behaviors. As you read "Mirror Image," use the chart to note details about the main character's traits. Think about how her traits influence events and affect the story's resolution.

Focus on Genre ❸
Short Story

- has a single idea and can be read in one sitting
- develops one or more characters
- presents a plot with one main conflict
- the setting often affects the plot
- may be realistic or imaginary
- often conveys a theme or lesson

Mirror Image

Short Story by Lena Coakley

? ESSENTIAL QUESTION:
What can blur the lines between what's real and what's not?

❶
Engage Your Brain

Choose one or more of these activities to start connecting with the short story you're about to read.

Myth or Reality?

Briefly research these statements about identical twins. Then, mark each as myth or reality. Share your findings with a partner.

- Identical twins always have identical fingerprints.
  Myth ☐   Reality ☐
- Identical twins can read each other's minds.
  Myth ☐   Reality ☐
- Identical twins don't always look identical.
  Myth ☐   Reality ☐

Me, Myself, and I

What makes you uniquely "you"? Complete one these sentences.

I'm happiest when _____ .

Three key words that describe me are _____ , _____ , and _____ .

My favorite place to be is _____ .

One thing I know for sure about myself is _____ .

"The eyes are the mirror(s) of the soul."

This proverb has been traced back to ancient times. It means that people's eyes reveal their true personality. Do you agree? Write down your thoughts.

❹ CHARACTER TRAITS	HOW TRAITS AFFECT PLOT
• physical appearance	
• speech, thoughts, and actions	
• others' impressions of the character and their interactions	

Mirror Image   **5**

❷ Introduce the **focus skills and standards** covered in the lesson.

❸ Review the **Focus on Genre** to familiarize students with characteristics of the genre before they read.

❹ Have your students use the **graphic organizers** to record key details, language, and ideas as they read.

Get Ready

Annotation in Action ⑤

Here is a note a student made about a section of "Mirror Image." As you read the selection, mark words related to character and setting, and note details that help you understand how characters respond to their situation.

> Alice had to re-learn how to move in the hospital, and to speak. At first the world was nothing but a mush of dark images, disconnected voices and prickly feelings all over her skin.
>
> *What has happened to Alice in the hospital?*

Expand Your Vocabulary

Put a check mark next to the vocabulary words that you feel comfortable using when speaking or writing.

⑥

- disquiet ☐
- prickly ☐
- mesmerize ☐
- adaptable ☐
- grimace ☐

Turn to a partner and talk about the vocabulary words you already know. Then, use as many of the words as you can in a 140-character post sharing your thoughts about being caught in a peculiar situation, one in which you may have had to check your reality. As you read "Mirror Image," use the definitions in the side column to learn the vocabulary words you don't already know.

Background ⑦

Born in Milford, Connecticut, **Lena Coakley** (b. 1967) credits her "larger-than-life" grandmother with providing the stability she needed as she grew up. Although she had little success with creative writing in high school, she studied writing while attending Sarah Lawrence College. Her first book was *Witchlanders*, a fantasy novel, followed by the adventure novel *Wicked Nix* and the historical-fiction fantasy *Worlds of Ink and Shadow: A Novel of the Brontës*. Now living in Toronto, Canada, Coakley has twice won second prize in the *Toronto Star's* short-story contest.

6   UNIT 1   ANALYZE & APPLY

---

⑤ As a class, discuss **Annotation in Action** to reinforce what effective close reading looks like.

⑥ See which **vocabulary words** students already know.

⑦ **Build background** about the author, setting, or topic.

⑧ Project the **Digital Student Edition** as you work through the activities as a class, or assign activities to small groups or individuals.

Get Ready

Analyze Character Traits

The **characters** in a short story are the people, animals, or imaginary creatures that take part in the action. Characters have personal qualities known as **character traits.** An author often describes characters' qualities and appearance directly, but just as often, a reader must figure out characters' traits based on their actions and behaviors. As you read "Mirror Image," use the chart to note details about the main character's traits. Think about how her traits influence events and affect the story's resolution.

⑧

Character Traits	How Traits Affect Plot
• physical appearance	
• speech, thoughts, and actions	
• others' impressions of the character and their interactions	

Teaching a Lesson: Read

❶ Use the **Notice & Note** annotations and questions to sharpen students' reading and text analysis. Learn more about the Notice & Note protocol on pages 66–71.

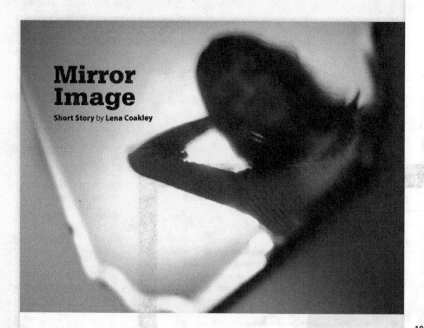

Mirror Image

Short Story by Lena Coakley

Being yourself is hard when you're a stranger.

NOTICE & NOTE

As you read, use the side margins to make notes about the text.

If only there were no mirrors, Alice sometimes thought, although she carried one in her backpack wherever she went. It was a silver-plated mirror her father had given her with the initials ACS on the back. Just you, Alice, she would say to herself, looking the way you've always looked. Then she'd pull out the mirror. The surprise and disbelief at seeing the reflection was a joke she played on herself over and over.

2 It was **disquieting**, however, to come upon a mirror without warning. She would say "excuse me" to her own reflection in shop windows. Mirrors in unexpected places would make her start and lose her nerve. She avoided the girls' bathroom altogether. Alice took to wearing sunglasses all the time, to remind herself, to keep something constantly in front of her eyes that would remind her that she looked different. Her teachers let her wear them. Maybe the word had come down from the top that she wasn't to be hassled for a while, but Alice

❷ ANALYZE CHARACTER TRAITS

Annotate: Review Jenny's description of Alice in paragraph 65. Mark any details that show Alice's current traits.

Analyze: What does Jenny's description reveal about her relationship with Alice at this point?

disquiet
(dis-kwī´-it) *tr.v.* Something that disquiets deprives someone of peace or rest.

Mirror Image **7**

---

❶ NOTICE & NOTE

TOUGH QUESTIONS

When you notice characters asking questions that reveal their internal struggles, you've found a **Tough Questions** signpost.

Notice & Note: In paragraph 22 underline the question Alice wonders about.

Analyze: What does this question make you wonder about?

mesmerize
(mĕz´mə-rīz´) *v.* To mesmerize someone is to spellbind them.

adaptable
(ə-dăp´tə-bəl) *adj.* Something that is adaptable can change or adjust to meet new conditions.

VOCABULARY

Suffixes: A **suffix** is a word part that appears at the end of a root or base word to form a new word. One meaning of the suffix *-able* is "inclined to a certain action." The word *unmistakable* also has the prefix *un-*, which means "not." The word *unmistakable* means "impossible to mistake or misinterpret."

Analyze: Why do you think the author notes that Alice's mother bears an unmistakable resemblance to Jenny?

20 "They couldn't have saved your old body," her mother said. "This was the only way to keep you alive."

21 "No one knows what it will be like," said Jenny. "You're the only one who's ever survived before."

22 "I know all that," Alice slurred. The doctors had taken the precaution of giving her a mild sedative.[2] It made her feel like everything was happening to someone else, far away. She held the silver mirror in one hand. With the other, she pulled at her face, squeezed it as if it were clay. Alice was **mesmerized** by the unfamiliar eyes, big and brown and dark. Whenever her father painted her, he'd spend most of his time on the eyes. The eyes are the mirror of the soul, he used to say. Whose soul is that? Alice wondered. For a moment she considered screaming, but it was too much trouble. Besides, it wouldn't be her scream.

23 "It's okay, Mom," she said. "Maybe I'll start looking like myself again. If I try hard enough. If I concentrate hard enough. Very slowly, over the course of years, my eyes will change color . . . my face. It might . . ."

24 Alice's mother stroked her hair. "We'll get through this," she said, "The human mind is incredibly **adaptable.**"

25 "Mrs. Jarred's on TV again," Alice called.

26 "Turn it off," her mother said, "It's time for birthday cake," but Alice and Jenny kept watching. Above the television, the faces of the family portrait Alice's father had painted smiled out into the room.

27 "A new development in the story of Girl X," said the newscaster, "first surviving recipient of a brain transplant . . ."

28 Alice's mother stood in the doorway wiping her hands on a tea towel. She had fewer freckles than Jenny, and the long braid which hung down her back wasn't quite so bright a red, but the family resemblance was unmistakable. "I don't want you to worry about the Jarreds, girls. My lawyer says they don't have a legal leg to stand on."

29 Mrs. Jarred, a middle-aged woman in a red checked coat, stood on a suburban lawn. She had dark hair just beginning to gray and Alice's large, dark eyes. A short man with a pot belly smiled self-consciously beside her.

30 "Is that your family?" Jenny asked.

31 "I don't even know them."

32 "Mrs. Jarred," said a female reporter with a microphone, "has science gone too far?"

33 "She's our daughter," the woman replied with emotion. "When we signed the release form donating her body, we

[2] **sedative:** a drug having a soothing, calming, or tranquilizing effect.

10 UNIT 1 ANALYZE & APPLY

❷ Have students answer the **Guided Reading Questions** in the margins to practice what they learned about the focus skills.

be better not to see you. It's very strange," he repeated, then added, "You look so different."

77   "I do?"

78   "Your hair. The way you stand, even. Our Gail, she was an early bloomer, always slouched. Your accent is different too." He paused. "I understand, you know. My wife, she thinks our daughter is still alive, but I. . . . I know." A car turned onto the street and honked at them. "I'd better go."

79   On impulse, Alice grabbed Mr. Jarred's hand. It was warm and big and rough, and Alice knew she had never felt it before. "I knew I wouldn't remember you," she said, "but I was hoping, when you walked by, that I'd know you somehow."

80   Mr. Jarred took his hand away. "But you don't."

81   "No." Alice slid her dark glasses to the top of her head. "My dad—I guess you know he died in the accident."

82   "Yes."

83   "Sometimes I think if he were alive, he would just look into my eyes and know who was in here."

84   The two stood in silence. Then Alice said, "What will you tell your wife?"

85   "I'll tell her," Mr. Jarred's voice began to falter, but he looked at her straight on, "I'll tell her I looked into your eyes and that I didn't see my daughter."

86   "I'm sorry," said Alice. She didn't ask the question that immediately came to her, but the words rang in her mind: who did you see?

87   Alice gripped the umbrella as she watched Mr. Jarred hurry around the corner. She stepped up to the curb and pressed her waist to the wooden barrier that protected the sidewalk. Then she folded the umbrella and secured the strap. In a small corner of the sidewalk she wrote her initials, ACS, with the tip of the umbrella.

88   Alice was here, she thought. And then she walked towards home.

?

ESSENTIAL QUESTION:

What can blur the lines between what's real and what's not?

4

Review your notes and add your thoughts to your Response Log.

3

TURN AND TALK

What is significant about the moment when Alice writes her initials in the cement? Discuss this moment with a partner.

3 Prompt meaningful discussion by using the **Turn and Talk** activity.

4 Have students revisit the **Essential Question**, recording evidence from the text in their Response Logs, which are located in the back of the Student Edition and online.

5 Use the **annotation and note-taking tools** in the eBook to model close reading and generate class discussion.

6 Check students' comprehension of the text with the **Assessment Practice** feature.

Assessment Practice

1. Read the excerpt from the story.

    "She put a large bite into her mouth. Bitter. Alice tried hard to swallow, tried hard not to let her face show a reaction to the cake, but the taste of the mocha forced her mouth into a grimace."

    (paragraph 53)

    What does the word *grimace* suggest about Alice?

    (A) She is desperate to amuse her mother and sister.

    (B) She is struggling to appear the same as always.

    (C) She is upset that her reaction shows she's not good at acting.

    (D) She is sorry she took a such a big bite of the cake.

2. This question has two parts. First answer **Part A**, then **Part B**.

    Part A

    How has Alice changed since her accident?

    (A) Her looks, tastes, and habits are no longer the same.

    (B) Her sense of right and wrong are very confused.

    (C) Her physical balance is less steady than it once was.

    (D) Her self-confidence is much stronger than before.

    Part B

    What is Alice trying to persuade her family to believe?

    (A) She is a better person than she was before the transplant.

    (B) She is aware her full recovery will take time.

    (C) She is not worried about the changes she is experiencing.

    (D) She is the same person she was before the transplant.

    ⊙Ed
    Test-Taking Strategies

© Houghton Mifflin Harcourt Publishing Company

manner that fully revealed her **apprehension** 💬. She was an apt woman; and a little experience soon demonstrated, to her satisfaction, that education and slavery were incompatible with each other.

3   From this time I was most narrowly watched. If I was in a separate room any ~~length of time, I was sure to~~ ~~be~~ aving a book, and was at ~~give~~ an account of myself. ~~It~~ was too late. The first ~~step~~ en. Mistress, in teaching ~~me~~ had given me the inch, ~~no~~ could prevent me from taking the *ell*.

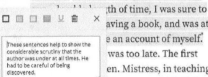

These sentences help to show the considerable scrutiny that the author was under at all times. He had to be careful of being discovered.

View in Panel   Save and Close

ANALYZE AUTOBIOGRAPHY

Annotate: Highlight details in paragraph 2 that describe Douglass's mistress.

Infer: Highlight *this* question text and add your responses as a note.

What might Douglass's purpose be in devoting so much space to describing his mistress?

15

Teaching a Lesson: Respond

Analyze the Text

Support your responses with evidence from the text.

① INTERPRET Consider the character traits of Alice's sister, Jenny, and their mother, whom you get to know primarily through their speech and actions. What do they seem to be feeling, based on their interactions with Alice? To check details, refer to the Character Traits chart you filled out as you read.

NOTICE & NOTE
Review what you **noticed and noted** as you read the text. Your annotations can help you answer these questions.

② SUMMARIZE How does the author use flashback to convey what happened to Alice?

③ ANALYZE Use this chart to record characters' descriptions of Alice at different points in the story.

CHARACTER	REFERS TO ALICE AS . . . (include paragraph number)	POSSIBLE REASON
Jenny		
Newscaster		
Mrs. Jarred		
Mr. Jarred		

④ INFER Alice and Jenny's father doesn't appear in the story; however, you learn many things about him. Describe what you understand about him based on story details.

⑤ DRAW CONCLUSIONS Recall that the climax of a story is its moment of greatest interest. What is the climax of "Mirror Image"? What details help you draw this conclusion?

⑥ EVALUATE How might the story be different if the author hadn't included **Memory Moments** through flashbacks?

⑦ ANALYZE Alice faces a lot of **Tough Questions** in the story. At one point her sister asks, "Who is to say that your whole personality is in your head?" After Alice's encounter with Mr. Jarred, how do you think she would respond to this question? Explain.

① Have students use their annotations to complete the Analyze the Text questions, which reinforce understanding of the focus skills.

② Use the Choices activities to extend students' analysis of the text. Find a range of options, including writing, media production, speaking and listening, research, and social and emotional learning.

② Choices

Here are some other ways to demonstrate your understanding of the ideas in this lesson.

Writing
▷ Diary Entry

Imagine that Alice returns home immediately from her encounter with Mr. Jarred to make an entry in her diary. Write a brief entry that details

- what she realizes about herself now
- what her attitude will be going forward

As you write and discuss, be sure to use the **Academic Vocabulary** words.

- abnormal
- feature
- focus
- perceive
- task

③

Speaking & Listening
▷ News Report

Imagine you're a newscaster covering Alice's story. Update viewers on the story by conducting a brief interview with Gail's parents, the Jarreds.

- Question Mr. Jarred about his meeting with Alice.
- Get Mrs. Jarred's response or opinion.
- Wrap up with a summary of your interview.

Social & Emotional Learning
▷ Turn a Mirror on Looks

Alice seems to like her new looks, but Jenny hints that Alice is being vain. Why do looks seem to matter so much in our society? Share your views with a small group.

- Discuss why social media has been called a "toxic mirror."
- Talk about the negative effects of making comparisons to or trying to live up to others' standards of beauty.
- Exchange advice on how to see ourselves in both realistic and positive terms.

③ Challenge students to use Academic Vocabulary in their writing and discussions.

④ Assign the Vocabulary Practice to help students master key words from the text.

⑤ Teach the Vocabulary Strategy, looking back at the text for context.

Expand Your Vocabulary ④

PRACTICE AND APPLY

With a partner, discuss and answer to each of the following questions. Then, work together to write sentences using each vocabulary word.

| disquiet | prickly | mesmerize | adaptable | grimace |

1. Which vocabulary word goes with *tingling?* Why?

2. Which vocabulary word goes with *fascinate?* Why?

3. Which vocabulary word goes with *uneasiness?* Why?

Vocabulary Strategy
 Suffixes *-able* and *-ible* ⑤

A **suffix** is a word part that appears at the end of a root or base word to form a new word. You can use your knowledge of suffixes to figure out word meanings. For example, look for a word with a suffix in this sentence from "Mirror Image."

The human mind is incredibly adaptable.

Note that *adaptable* is made up of the base word *adapt* and the suffix *-able*. The suffixes *-able* and *-ible* mean "capable of or worthy of." Therefore, *adaptable* means "capable of change."

Underline the suffix in each boldface word. Then, write the word's meaning.

1. People's behavior is **changeable** because life experiences can influence thoughts, feelings, and actions.

2. It is **regrettable** when twin sisters act like strangers.

3. The cake was **digestible,** but it was not very tasty.

Ed
Interactive Vocabulary Lesson: Common Roots, Prefixes, and Suffixes

18   UNIT 1 ANALYZE

Watch Your Language! ⑥

Punctuating Dialogue

Dialogue is the words spoken by or between characters. It's important to punctuate dialogue correctly so that readers understand what each character says. Here are some rules for punctuating story dialogue.

● Use quotation marks to enclose a direct quotation—a character's exact words.

"Let me read your diary."

● Direct quotations usually begin with an uppercase letter. However, when the speaker interrupts a quoted sentence, the second part of the quotation begins with a lowercase letter.

"By two minutes," said Jenny, "and anyway, maybe I'm not the oldest anymore."

● A period or a comma is always placed inside the closing quotation marks. The same is true of a question mark or exclamation point unless it is not part of the quotation.

"Mrs. Jarred," said a female reporter with a microphone, "has science gone too far?"

PRACTICE AND APPLY ⑦

Rewrite each sentence to correct the punctuation errors.

Ed
Grammar Practice: Quotation Marks

1. "Where did my diary go"? he asked. "It was just here."

2. "I think I might have knocked it down," she said, "When I reached for the remote."

3. "You're right," he confirmed. "it fell on the carpet."

4. "Did I hear you say 'You're right?'" she asked.

⑥ Use the Watch Your Language! feature to teach grammar in context.

⑦ Assign the Practice and find more practice online.

Mirror Image   19

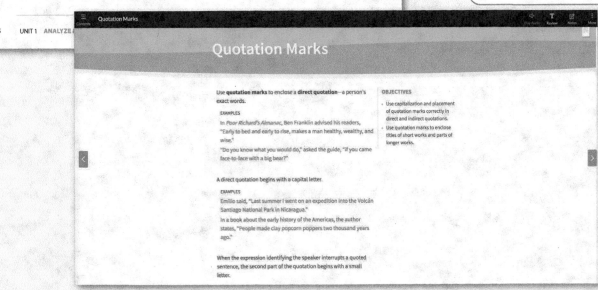

Adapting
Into Literature

Teacher's Edition

No two educators will approach *Into Literature* in the same way. You can customize what's here to work for you, your school, and most importantly, your students. The articles in the next section of this guide will help you adapt this program to your needs. Here is a preview of some of the core and supporting resources that allow for flexibility and choice, starting with your Teacher's Edition.

Unit Planning Guides

All the **Unit Planning Guides** for your grade level are available in the back of this guide, on pages 146–181. Consult these materials as you plan and adapt your curriculum for the unit or year.

Instructional Features:

1. Find information about **realistic pacing** and **text complexity** for each lesson in the unit.

2. View **standards** covered in each lesson.

3. Discover **online resources** to support your instruction.

4. Preview **independent reading options** connected to the unit.

5. See **options for assessing mastery** of unit standards and skills.

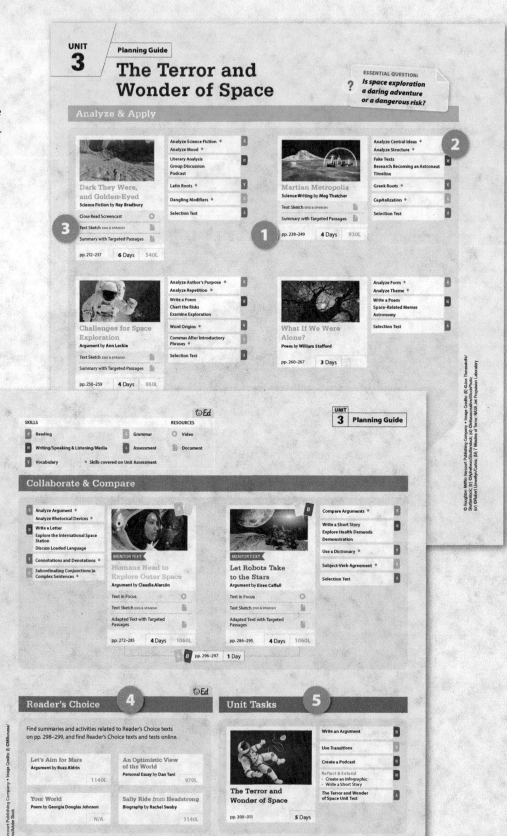

Want specific ideas for integrating longer works into your teaching? Find practical suggestions and resources on pages 48–51.

Instructional Features:

6 Discover **Short Reads** that connect to the unit, should you want to make any changes to the default lessons or texts.

7 Use the tips to find instructional resources that can pair with these texts.

8 Use the **Long Reads** suggestions to help you integrate novels and other longer works into the unit. You will find five recommendations for each unit.

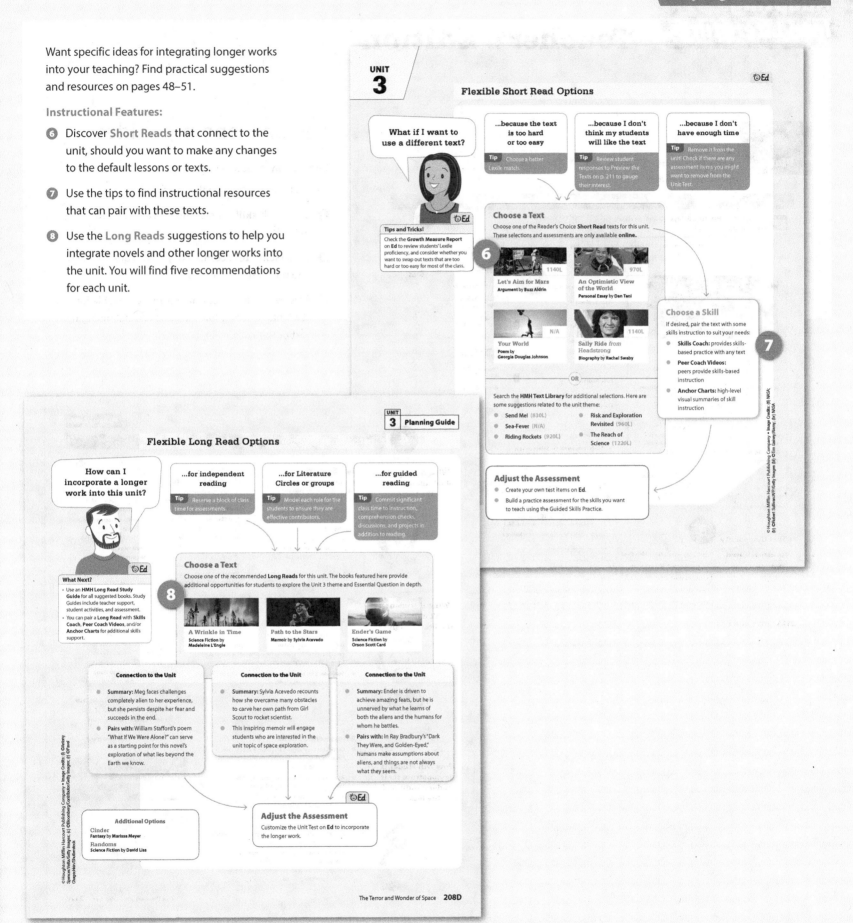

UNIT 3

Flexible Short Read Options

What if I want to use a different text?

Tips and Tricks!
Check the **Growth Measure Report** on **Ed** to review students' Lexile proficiency, and consider whether you want to swap out texts that are too hard or too easy for most of the class.

...because the text is too hard or too easy
Tip Choose a better Lexile match.

...because I don't think my students will like the text
Tip Review student responses to Preview the Texts on p. 211 to gauge their interest.

...because I don't have enough time
Tip Remove it from the unit! Check if there are any assessment items you might want to remove from the Unit Test.

Choose a Text
Choose one of the Reader's Choice **Short Read** texts for this unit. These selections and assessments are only available **online**.

6
Let's Aim for Mars — Argument by Buzz Aldrin — 1140L
An Optimistic View of the World — Personal Essay by Dan Tani — 970L
Your World — Poem by Georgia Douglas Johnson — N/A
Sally Ride from Headstrong — Biography by Rachel Swaby — 1140L

OR

Search the **HMH Text Library** for additional selections. Here are some suggestions related to the unit theme:
- Send Me! (830L)
- Sea-Fever (N/A)
- Riding Rockets (920L)
- Risk and Exploration Revisited (960L)
- The Reach of Science (1220L)

Choose a Skill
If desired, pair the text with some skills instruction to suit your needs:
- **Skills Coach:** provides skills-based practice with any text
- **Peer Coach Videos:** peers provide skills-based instruction
- **Anchor Charts:** high-level visual summaries of skill instruction

7

Adjust the Assessment
- Create your own test items on **Ed**.
- Build a practice assessment for the skills you want to teach using the Guided Skills Practice.

UNIT 3 Planning Guide

Flexible Long Read Options

How can I incorporate a longer work into this unit?

What Next?
- Use an **HMH Long Read Study Guide** for all suggested books. Study Guides include teacher support, student activities, and assessment.
- You can pair a **Long Read** with Skills Coach, Peer Coach Videos, and/or Anchor Charts for additional skills support.

...for independent reading
Tip Reserve a block of class time for assessments.

...for Literature Circles or groups
Tip Model each role for the students to ensure they are effective contributors.

...for guided reading
Tip Commit significant class time to instruction, comprehension checks, discussions, and projects in addition to reading.

Choose a Text
Choose one of the recommended **Long Reads** for this unit. The books featured here provide additional opportunities for students to explore the Unit 3 theme and Essential Question in depth.

8

A Wrinkle in Time — Science Fiction by Madeleine L'Engle
Path to the Stars — Memoir by Sylvia Acevedo
Ender's Game — Science Fiction by Orson Scott Card

Connection to the Unit
- **Summary:** Meg faces challenges completely alien to her experience, but she persists despite her fear and succeeds in the end.
- **Pairs with:** William Stafford's poem "What If We Were Alone?" can serve as a starting point for this novel's exploration of what lies beyond the Earth we know.

Connection to the Unit
- **Summary:** Sylvia Acevedo recounts how she overcame many obstacles to carve her own path from Girl Scout to rocket scientist.
- This inspiring memoir will engage students who are interested in the unit topic of space exploration.

Connection to the Unit
- **Summary:** Ender is driven to achieve amazing feats, but he is unnerved by what he learns of both the aliens and the humans for whom he battles.
- **Pairs with:** In Ray Bradbury's "Dark They Were, and Golden-Eyed," humans make assumptions about aliens, and things are not always what they seem.

Additional Options
Cinder — Fantasy by Marissa Meyer
Randoms — Science Fiction by David Liss

Adjust the Assessment
Customize the Unit Test on **Ed** to incorporate the longer work.

The Terror and Wonder of Space **208D**

Adapting *Into Literature*

Teacher's Edition

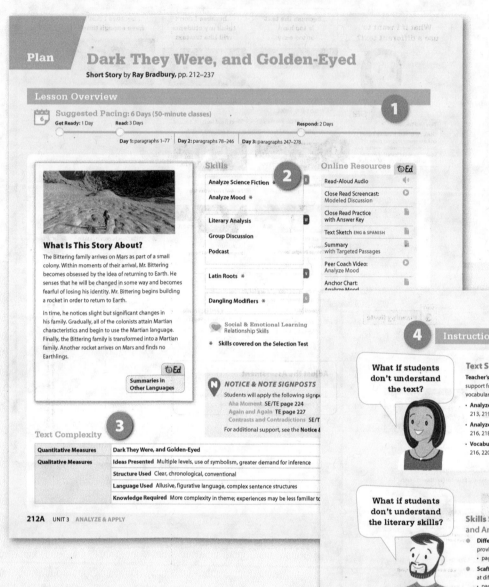

Lesson Planning Guides

Instructional Features:

1. Learn more about **realistic pacing**.

2. See which **skills and standards** are covered in the lesson.

3. Understand **text complexity**—both quantitative and qualitative measures.

4. Preview the **Instructional Support** available for students who may have trouble understanding the text or the skills.

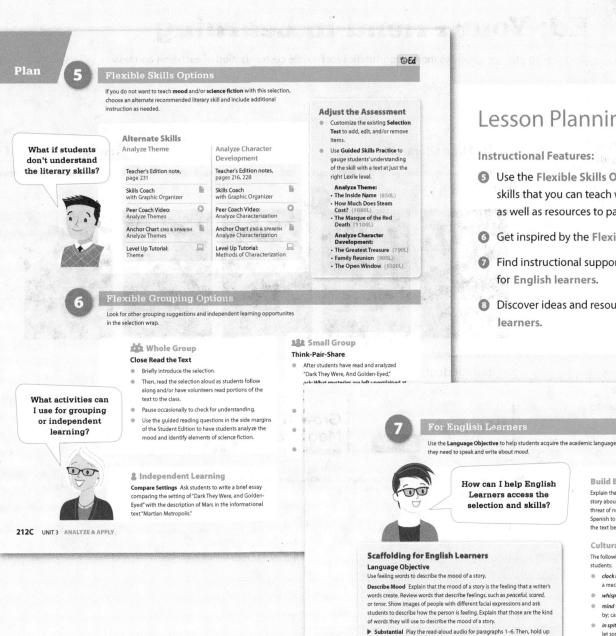

Plan ❺ Flexible Skills Options

If you do not want to teach **mood** and/or **science fiction** with this selection, choose an alternate recommended literary skill and include additional instruction as needed.

> **What if students don't understand the literary skills?**

Alternate Skills

Analyze Theme

Teacher's Edition note, page 231

Skills Coach
with Graphic Organizer

Peer Coach Video:
Analyze Themes

Anchor Chart ENG & SPANISH
Analyze Themes

Level Up Tutorial:
Theme

Analyze Character Development

Teacher's Edition notes, pages 216, 22B

Skills Coach
with Graphic Organizer

Peer Coach Video:
Analyze Characterization

Anchor Chart ENG & SPANISH
Analyze Characterization

Level Up Tutorial:
Methods of Characterization

Adjust the Assessment

● Customize the existing **Selection Test** to add, edit, and/or remove items.

● Use **Guided Skills Practice** to gauge students' understanding of the skill with a text at just the right Lexile level.

Analyze Theme:
• The Inside Name (850L)
• How Much Does Steam Cost? (1080L)
• The Masque of the Red Death (1100L)

Analyze Character Development:
• The Greatest Treasure (790L)
• Family Reunion (900L)
• The Open Window (1020L)

❻ Flexible Grouping Options

Look for other grouping suggestions and independent learning opportunites in the selection wrap.

> **What activities can I use for grouping or independent learning?**

👥 Whole Group

Close Read the Text

● Briefly introduce the selection.

● Then, read the selection aloud as students follow along and/or have volunteers read portions of the text to the class.

● Pause occasionally to check for understanding.

● Use the guided reading questions in the side margins of the Student Edition to have students analyze the mood and identify elements of science fiction.

👥 Small Group

Think-Pair-Share

● After students have read and analyzed "Dark They Were, And Golden-Eyed,"
ask: What mysteries are left unexplained at

🧑 Independent Learning

Compare Settings Ask students to write a brief essay comparing the setting of "Dark They Were, and Golden-Eyed" with the description of Mars in the informational text "Martian Metropolis."

212C UNIT 3 ANALYZE & APPLY

Lesson Planning Guides

Instructional Features:

❺ Use the **Flexible Skills Options** for ideas on additional skills that you can teach with the text, as well as resources to pair for instruction.

❻ Get inspired by the **Flexible Grouping Options**.

❼ Find instructional support and additional practice for **English learners**.

❽ Discover ideas and resources for challenging **advanced learners**.

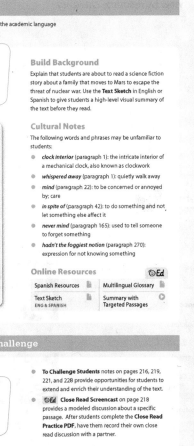

Planning Guide

❼ For English Learners

Use the **Language Objective** to help students acquire the academic language they need to speak and write about *mood*.

> **How can I help English Learners access the selection and skills?**

Scaffolding for English Learners

Language Objective
Use feeling words to describe the mood of a story.

Describe Mood Explain that the mood of a story is the feeling that a writer's words create. Review words that describe feelings, such as *peaceful, scared,* or *tense*. Show images of people with different facial expressions and ask students to describe how the person is feeling. Explain that those are the kind of words they will use to describe the mood of a story.

▶ **Substantial** Play the read-aloud audio for paragraphs 1–6. Then, hold up the **Text Sketch** and ask students how the family arrives on Mars. (*on a rocket*) Then, ask them to use a feeling word to describe how the father acts after he gets off of the rocket. (*scared*)

▶ **Moderate** Have students reread paragraph 8 aloud. (Point out the cognates *disolver* and *intelecto*.) Ask: What is the father afraid of losing? (*his ability to think logically*) Describe the mood the father's fear helps create. (*fearful, tense*)

▶ **Light** Have partners retell the events in paragraphs 1–8 to each other. Ask them to identify words in the text that help create the story's mood.

Build Background

Explain that students are about to read a science fiction story about a family that moves to Mars to escape the threat of nuclear war. Use the **Text Sketch** in English or Spanish to give students a high-level visual summary of the text before they read.

Cultural Notes

The following words and phrases may be unfamiliar to students:

● *clock interior* (paragraph 1): the intricate interior of a mechanical clock, also known as clockwork

● *whispered away* (paragraph 1): quietly walk away

● *mind* (paragraph 22): to be concerned or annoyed by; care

● *in spite of* (paragraph 42): to do something and not let something else affect it

● *never mind* (paragraph 165): used to tell someone to forget something

● *hadn't the foggiest notion* (paragraph 270): expression for not knowing something

Online Resources

Spanish Resources	Multilingual Glossary
Text Sketch ENG & SPANISH	Summary with Targeted Passages

❽ For Students Who Need a Challenge

> **How do I support students who need a challenge?**

● **To Challenge Students** notes on pages 216, 219, 221, and 22B provide opportunities for students to extend and enrich their understanding of the text.

● **Close Read Screencast** on page 218 provides a modeled discussion about a specific passage. After students complete the **Close Read Practice PDF**, have them record their own close read discussion with a partner.

Dark They Were, and Golden-Eyed **212D**

Ed: Your Friend in Learning

Our learning platform provides more opportunities for flexible customization of each unit and lesson.

 Use our online tools to choose your path through *Into Literature*.

Browse Program Resources

① **Preview resources** by browsing the units and lessons in the program structure, or choose to view by resource category.

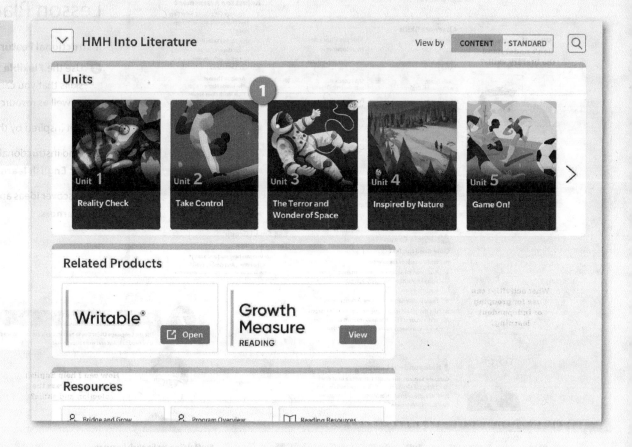

Find Content Your Students Need

② Find instructional resources to support the teaching of the content you love. Search by **selection, skill, or keyword,** and use the Component filter as you browse to refine your search.

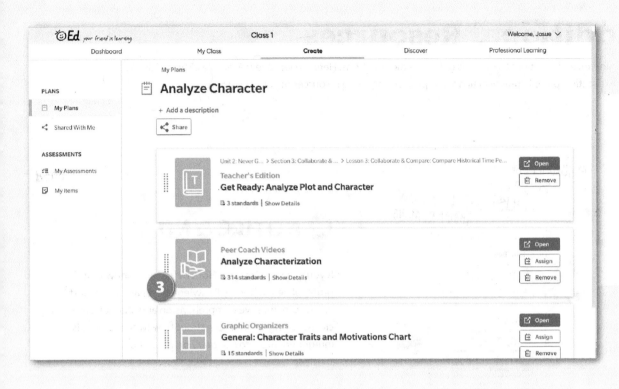

Create Your Own Lesson Plans

❸ **Create your own lesson plans** for each unit. Lessons can become your shortcut to the resources you want to use.

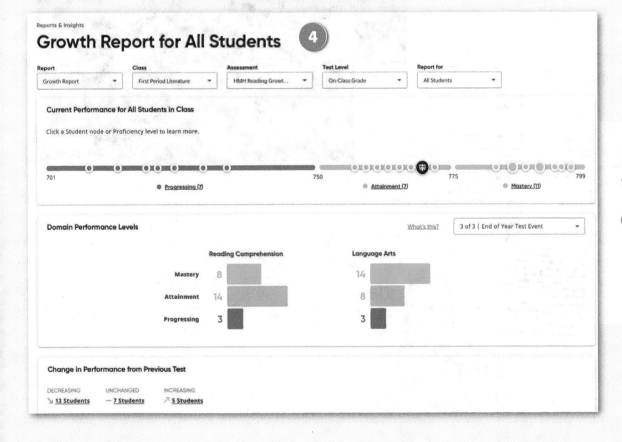

Differentiate with Data

❹ Use the **HMH Growth Measure** or **Standards Report** to drive your planning and differentiation decisions. Learn more on pages 118–119.

Additional Resources

An abundance of additional resources gives you more options. Here are just a few examples. The articles in the next section provide practical tips for implementing these resources in your classroom.

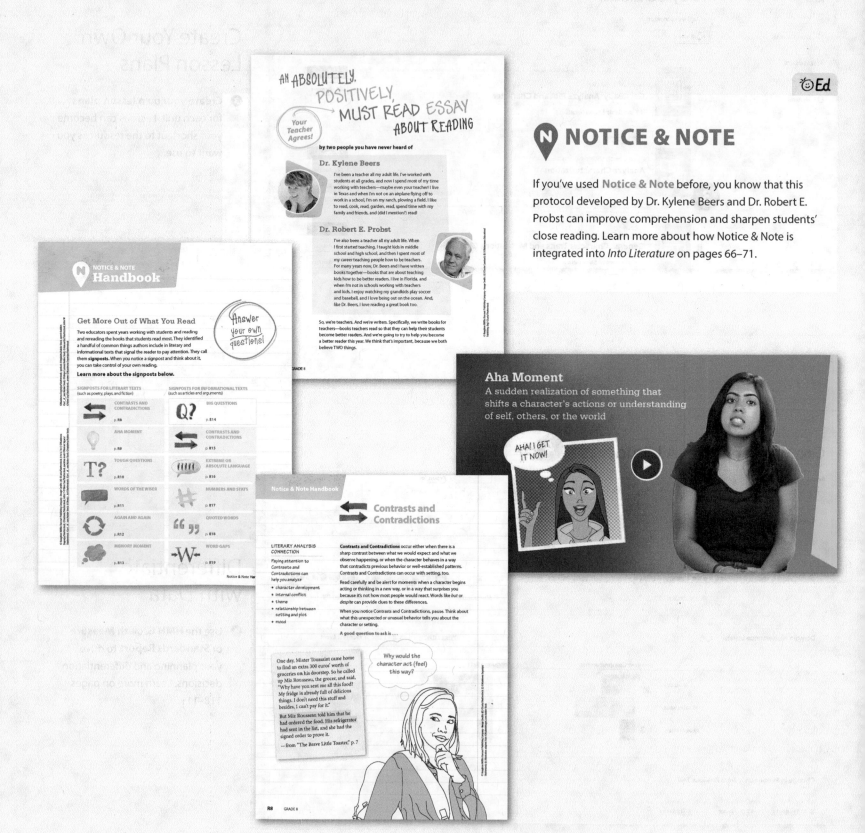

⊕ Ed

AN *ABSOLUTELY,*
POSITIVELY,
→ MUST READ ESSAY
ABOUT READING

Your Teacher Agrees!

by two people you have never heard of

Dr. Kylene Beers

I've been a teacher all my adult life. I've worked with students at all grades, and now I spend most of my time working with teachers—maybe even your teacher! I live in Texas and when I'm not on an airplane flying off to work in a school, I'm on my ranch, plowing a field. I like to read, cook, read, garden, read, spend time with my family and friends, and (did I mention?) read!

Dr. Robert E. Probst

I've also been a teacher all my adult life. When I first started teaching, I taught kids in middle school and high school, and then I spent most of my career teaching people how to be teachers. For many years now, Dr. Beers and I have written books together—books that are about teaching kids how to be better readers. I live in Florida, and when I'm not in schools working with teachers and kids, I enjoy watching my grandkids play soccer and baseball, and I love being out on the ocean. And, like Dr. Beers, I love reading a great book too.

So, we're teachers. And we're writers. Specifically, we write books for teachers—books teachers read so that they can help their students become better readers. And we're going to try to help you become a better reader this year. We think that's important, because we both believe TWO things.

NOTICE & NOTE

If you've used **Notice & Note** before, you know that this protocol developed by Dr. Kylene Beers and Dr. Robert E. Probst can improve comprehension and sharpen students' close reading. Learn more about how Notice & Note is integrated into *Into Literature* on pages 66–71.

NOTICE & NOTE
Handbook

Get More Out of What You Read

Two educators spent years working with students and reading and rereading the books that students read most. They identified a handful of common things authors include in literary and informational texts that signal the reader to pay attention. They call them **signposts.** When you notice a signpost and think about it, you can take control of your own reading.

Learn more about the signposts below.

Answer your own questions!

SIGNPOSTS FOR LITERARY TEXTS
(such as poetry, plays, and fiction)

CONTRASTS AND CONTRADICTIONS p. R8	
AHA MOMENT p. R9	
TOUGH QUESTIONS p. R10	
WORDS OF THE WISER p. R11	
AGAIN AND AGAIN p. R12	
MEMORY MOMENT p. R13	

SIGNPOSTS FOR INFORMATIONAL TEXTS
(such as articles and arguments)

Q? BIG QUESTIONS p. R14	
CONTRASTS AND CONTRADICTIONS p. R15	
EXTREME OR ABSOLUTE LANGUAGE p. R16	
NUMBERS AND STATS p. R17	
QUOTED WORDS p. R18	
W WORD GAPS p. R19	

Notice & Note Ha

Aha Moment
A sudden realization of something that shifts a character's actions or understanding of self, others, or the world

AHA! I GET IT NOW!

Notice & Note Handbook

Contrasts and Contradictions

LITERARY ANALYSIS CONNECTION

Paying attention to *Contrasts and Contradictions* can help you analyze

• character development
• internal conflict
• theme
• relationship between setting and plot
• mood

Contrasts and Contradictions occur either when there is a sharp contrast between what we would expect and what we observe happening, or when the character behaves in a way that contradicts previous behavior or well-established patterns. Contrasts and Contradictions can occur with setting, too.

Read carefully and be alert for moments when a character begins acting or thinking in a new way, or in a way that surprises you because it's not how most people would react. Words like *but* or *despite* can provide clues to these differences.

When you notice Contrasts and Contradictions, pause. Think about what this unexpected or unusual behavior tells you about the character or setting.

A good question to ask is . . .

One day, Mister Toussaint came home to find an extra 300 euros' worth of groceries on his doorstep. So he called up Miz Rousseau, the grocer, and said, "Why have you sent me all this food? My fridge is already full of delicious things. I don't need this stuff and besides, I can't pay for it."

But Miz Rousseau told him that he had ordered the food. His refrigerator had sent in the list, and she had the signed order to prove it.

—from "The Brave Little Toaster," p. 7

Why would the character act (feel) this way?

R8   GRADE 8

Resources for Differentiation

The range of readers and abilities in your classroom can run the gamut. Armed with the right resources for **differentiation**, you can meet the many needs your students have. Find tips for differentiating instruction and uncover just the right resources to do that effectively on pages 100–111.

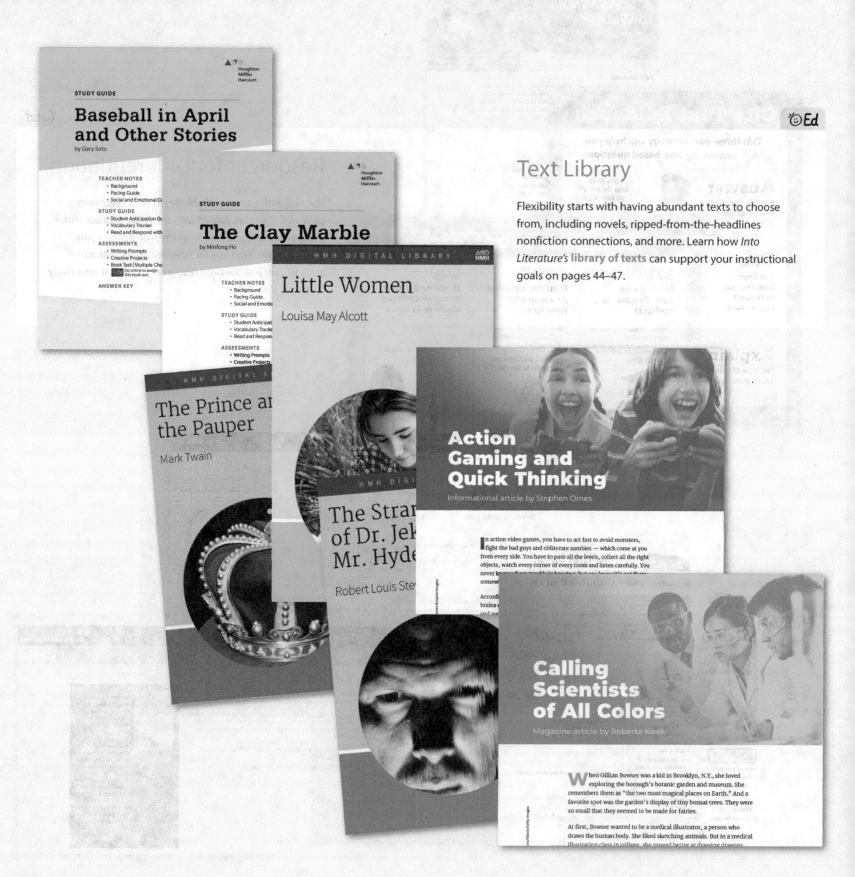

STUDY GUIDE

Baseball in April and Other Stories

by Gary Soto

TEACHER NOTES
- Background
- Pacing Guide
- Social and Emotional C...

STUDY GUIDE
- Student Anticipation Gu...
- Vocabulary Tracker
- Read and Respond with...

ASSESSMENTS
- Writing Prompts
- Creative Projects
- Book Test (Multiple Cho...)
  Go online to assign this book test.

ANSWER KEY

STUDY GUIDE

The Clay Marble

by Minfong Ho

TEACHER NOTES
- Background
- Pacing Guide
- Social and Emotio...

STUDY GUIDE
- Student Anticipat...
- Vocabulary Tracke...
- Read and Respon...

ASSESSMENTS
- Writing Prompts
- Creative Projects

HMH DIGITAL LIBRARY

Little Women

Louisa May Alcott

HMH DIGITAL L...

The Prince an... the Pauper

Mark Twain

HMH DIG...

The Stran... of Dr. Jek... Mr. Hyde

Robert Louis Stev...

Action Gaming and Quick Thinking

Informational article by Stephen Ornes

In action video games, you have to act fast to avoid monsters, fight the bad guys and obliterate zombies — which come at you from every side. You have to pass all the levels, collect all the right objects, watch every corner of every room and listen carefully. You never kn... ... ...

Accordi... brains ... and an...

Calling Scientists of All Colors

Magazine article by Roberta Kwok

When Gillian Bowser was a kid in Brooklyn, N.Y., she loved exploring the borough's botanic garden and museum. She remembers them as "the two most magical places on Earth." And a favorite spot was the garden's display of tiny bonsai trees. They were so small that they seemed to be made for fairies.

At first, Bowser wanted to be a medical illustrator, a person who draws the human body. She liked sketching animals. But in a medical illustration class in college, she proved better at drawing dragons

Text Library

Flexibility starts with having abundant texts to choose from, including novels, ripped-from-the-headlines nonfiction connections, and more. Learn how *Into Literature's* library of texts can support your instructional goals on pages 44–47.

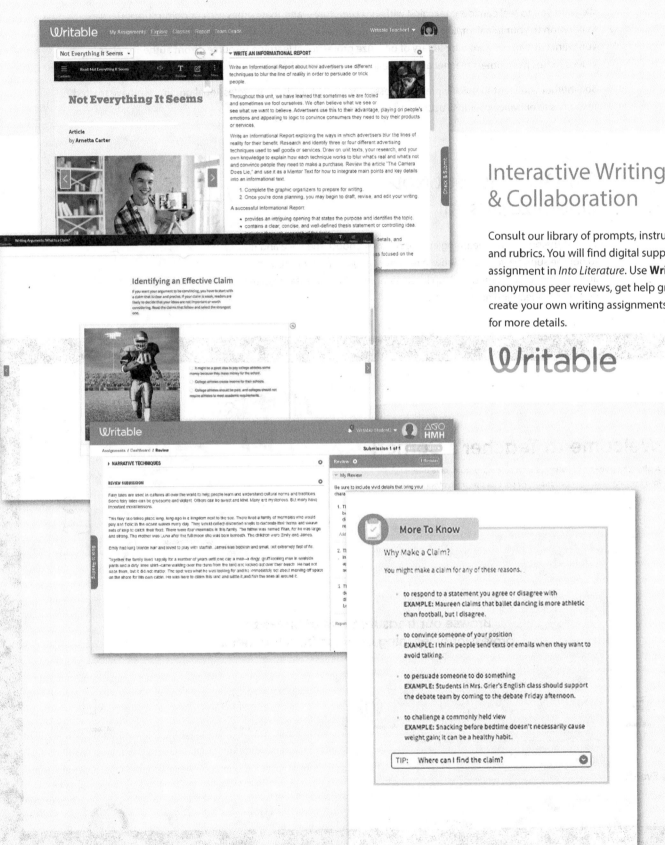

Interactive Writing & Collaboration

Consult our library of prompts, instructional supports, and rubrics. You will find digital support for each writing assignment in *Into Literature*. Use **Writable** to facilitate anonymous peer reviews, get help grading essays, or create your own writing assignments. See pages 78–83 for more details.

Writable

Teacher's Corner

We want you to feel confident teaching with *Into Literature*—and that comes with ongoing support. In addition to your initial implementation of professional learning, **Teacher's Corner** gives you the support you want with an ever-growing library of bite-size professional learning resources, from authentic class videos to tips from others teacher and our team of experienced coaches.

So whether you want to quickly prep for a lesson or invest time in your professional growth, we have trusted resources to enhance your instruction and class tomorrow.

On-Demand, But Not One-Size-Fits-All

We put the professional learning in your hands—choose the pace and time to get the support you need. Browse resources aligned to your programs and beyond to get started, pick up implementation tips, and stay inspired with lesson ideas and new research.

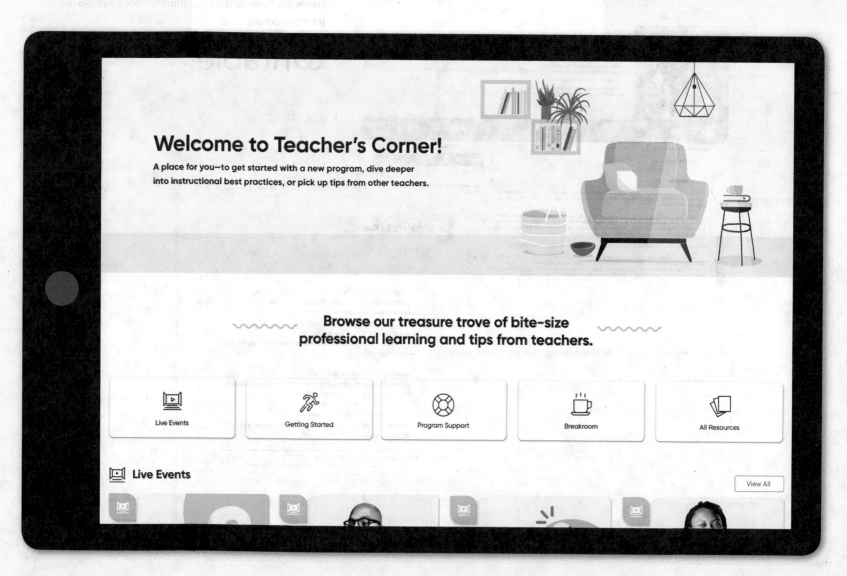

Welcome to Teacher's Corner!

A place for you—to get started with a new program, dive deeper into instructional best practices, or pick up tips from other teachers.

Browse our treasure trove of bite-size professional learning and tips from teachers.

| Live Events | Getting Started | Program Support | Breakroom | All Resources |

Live Events　　　　　　　　　　　　　　　View All

Curated, Trusted Content

There's no shortage of free resources online, but with Teacher's Corner, professional learning and instructional recommendations align to best practices. Hear exclusively from prominent thought leaders, experienced coaches, and practicing teachers.

Ready & Relevant for Tomorrow's Instruction

Designed to be practical and applicable to planning and teaching, Teacher's Corner includes authentic class videos, expert videos, interactive articles, and podcasts.

A Community of Live Support

Our Live Events give you exclusive access to extend your learning by connecting with our instructional coaches, thought leaders, and each other.

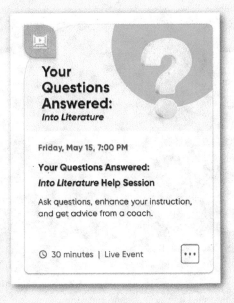

Flexibility & Choice

Planning the Year

Explore Six Thematic Units

With its deliberate instructional design, *Into Literature* moves students from guided whole-class instruction to small-group peer collaboration to independence. Here is an overview of the key features in each unit.

What have you given me to work with?

⊙ Ed

Unit Opener

- 2–3 engagement activities to help students connect to the unit theme

Analyze & Apply

- 2–4 lessons, each with an accompanying **Selection Test**
- 1 or 2 **Mentor Texts**, authentic examples of the type of writing students will do at the end of the unit

Collaborate & Compare

- 1–2 text groupings so students can think critically across related texts, with an accompanying **Selection Test**

Reader's Choice

- 4–6 short read recommendations for independent reading with an accompanying **Selection Test**

- 3 long read recommendations for independent reading, with an accompanying **Book Test**

End-of-Unit Tasks

- 1 writing assignment
- 1 speaking & listening assignment
- 1 media project
- 1 **Unit Test**

Additional Support

Text Library

- Texts across different genres and Lexile® ranges
- Digital novels and nonfiction texts
- Printable **Reader's Choice** texts
- HMH Study Guides and assessments

Text Support

- **Adapted Texts and Summaries**, and **Text Sketch** overviews to support struggling readers and English learners
- **Notice & Note Anchor Charts** to support close reading
- **Multilingual Glossaries**, with terms in 10 languages
- **Spanish Unit Resources**
- **Text in Focus Videos and Practice** to focus deeply on a specific text element
- **Close Read Screencasts and Practice** to model what close reading sounds like

Skills Support

- **Anchor Charts** for high level skills instruction
- **Peer Coach Videos**, in which students can learn from their peers
- **Guided Skills Practice**, providing targeted skills practice paired with texts at a range of Lexile® levels for just the right fit
- **Level Up Tutorials and Practice Tests** for independent practice and remediation
- **Interactive Writing, Grammar, Vocabulary**, and **Speaking & Listening Lessons** for additional practice
- **Media Projects** connected to each unit theme

Analyze Characterization

What does the character look like?

What is his or her personality like?

What does the character think, say, and do?

What do other...

Characters are... tells you abou... guess from the...

MARTIAN METROPOLIS
TEXT SKETCH
Science Writing by Meg Thacher

COLONIZE = make a home in a distant place   METROPOLIS = a large city

NASA will send humans to colonize Mars.

WHY WILL IT WORK?
Mars is the planet most like Earth.

WHY WILL IT BE HARD?
- Mars is much colder than Earth.
- There is a risk of radiation.
- Travel will be difficult.

HOW WILL THEY DO IT?
Settlers will need to provide their own food, shelter, and energy.

How else will life on Mars be different?

Getting to Know *Into Literature*

Pick and Choose

Into Literature includes more than 180 days of instruction, which means you have plenty of options. Where you choose to spend time and what you choose to set aside will affect your overall pacing, but we've provided supports in the Teacher's Edition to help you make these decisions.

Can I really do all of this in one year?

- Use the pacing recommendations for each Unit Opener so you can gauge about how much time it will take to introduce a unit. Spend additional time on background and engagement activities or skip them entirely.

- Consult the **Lesson Planning Guide** for each text to find realistic pacing suggestions for pre-teaching, reading, and post-reading activities and instruction. Consider these a starting point for pacing, as you think through how much you can cover within the academic year.

1 INTRODUCE THE UNIT: **1 day**

Set the Stage

▶ Introduce the unit by playing the **Stream to Start** video.

Suggested Pacing: 6 Days (50 minute classes)

Get Ready: 1 Day   **Read:** 3 Days   **Respond:** 2 Days

Day 1: paragraphs 1–77 | **Day 2:** paragraphs 78–246 | **Day 3:** paragraphs 247–278

- **Ed** If you follow a benchmark of nine weeks per unit, you might choose to include only four of the six units. You can easily piece together "gap lessons" to address any additional standards or skills by using our **Anchor Charts**, **Peer Coach Videos**, and **Skills Coach** resources, all available on our learning platform.

- Another factor that will affect your pacing is how much class time students will spend working through readings and assignments. Should you decide to do much of the reading in class, instead of assigning it as homework, you'll need to build in more time. The same would apply for the end-of-unit writing task—if you prefer to have students completing this assignment in class, this will require additional time.

Suggested Pacing: 5 Days (50 minute classes)

What if I want to organize the units in other ways?

Tips & Tricks!

Creating custom digital plans on our learning platform will help you keep track of exactly the resources you want to use, and manage who gets which resources. You can also share your custom plans with peers and administrators.

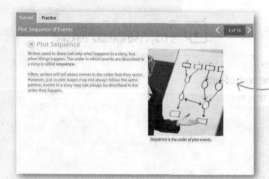

Sequence is the order of plot events.

Go For It!

We have organized our units thematically, but *Into Literature* is flexible enough to support what you need, whether your district plans and delivers curriculum to you, or you are building it yourself or with a team.

- **Building units around standards?** No problem. You can use our learning platform to browse content by your state's standards. Then use filters to hone in on the kind of resources you're looking for.

- **Incorporating novels into your curriculum?** That works too. Consult the suggested long reads connected to each unit, as well as the accompanying **HMH Study Guide** and digital assessment online.

- **Crafting units around genres?** You've got it. The Student Edition includes a Table of Contents by genre. Online, you can browse either the Student Edition or Teacher's Edition and use the genre filter to check out the range of texts available with our embedded instructional supports. You also can find additional text options in the **Text Library**.

- **Need skills instruction to support your texts?** You can easily incorporate additional instructional resources to pair with any texts you've added. The following resources are waiting for you on the platform:

  - **Anchor Charts:** High-level visual summaries of skills and ideas
  - **Peer Coach Videos:** Videos of students' peers teaching skills
  - **Skills Coach:** Skills-based graphic organizers that can be paired with any text
  - **Level Up Tutorials and Practice Tests:** Skills-based remediation lessons for independent learning

Teaching the Standards

> ## How can I make sure I have covered all of my state's standards?

We've Got You

Consult these program resources as you formulate your instructional plans at the beginning of the year.

- ☺**Ed** Find the lesson that you want to teach on Ed. Each text is tagged to your state standards.

- ☺**Ed** As the year progresses and you want to teach a specific standard, use the Filter by Standards on Ed to find a text.

- You can also refer to the **Unit Planning Guides** in the Teacher's Edition and at the end of this Program Guide to see the skills coverage for each unit. See pages 146–181.

- ☺**Ed** Pair our online **Skills Coach** resources with texts you're trying to teach to meet tricky-to-cover standards.

UNIT 1 | Planning Guide

Gadgets and Glitches

ESSENTIAL QUESTION: Does technology improve or control our lives?

Analyze & Apply

The Brave Little Toaster
Science Fiction by Cory Doctorow
- Analyze Plot
- Analyze Science Fiction
- Summarize a Story
- Discuss with a Small Group
- Create a Comic
- Context Clues
- Participles
- Selection Test

Text Sketch ENG & SPANISH
Summary with Targeted Passages
pp. 4–15 · 5 Days · 990L

Are Bionic Superhumans on the Horizon?
Informational Text by Ramez Naam
- Identify Central Ideas and Details
- Analyze Organization
- Informative Essay
- Discuss with a Small Group
- Create a Graphic Aid
- Synonyms and Antonyms
- Commonly Confused Words
- Selection Test

Text Sketch ENG & SPANISH
Summary with Targeted Passages
Text in Focus
pp. 16–27 · 4 Days · 1110L

Interflora
Poem by Susan Hamlyn
- Analyze Structure
- Analyze Irony
- Sonnet
- Present a Sonnet
- Design a Virtual Bouquet
- Selection Test

pp. 28–35 · 3 Days · N/A

SKILLS
- R Reading
- W Writing/Speaking & Listening/Media
- V Vocabulary
- G Grammar
- A Assessment
- ✳ Skills covered on Unit Assessment

RESOURCES
- Video
- Document

☺**Ed**

Collaborate & Compare

The Automation Paradox
Argument by James Bessen
- Analyze Claim and Evidence
- Analyze Graphic Features
- Argue It
- Prepare for the Future
- Use a Dictionary
- Transitional Words and Phrases

MENTOR TEXT
Close Read Screencast
pp. 36–49 · 5 Days · 1140L

Heads Up, Humans
Argument by Claudia Alarcón
- Evaluate Evidence
- Analyze Rhetoric
- Compare Arguments
- Create a Public Service Announcement
- Discuss with a Small Group
- My Future Job
- Use Greek Roots
- Active and Passive Voice
- Selection Test

MENTOR TEXT
pp. 50–61 · 4 Days · 1300L

pp. 62–63 · 1 Day

☺**Ed**

Reader's Choice

Find summaries and activities related to Reader's Choice texts on pp. 64–65 and find Reader's Choice texts and tests online.

If You Go into the Woods You will Find It Has a Technology
Poem by Meather Christle · N/A

Hallucination
Science Fiction by Isaac Asimov · 790L

There Will Come Soft Rains
Science Fiction by Ray Bradbury · 880L

from All the Light We Cannot See
Novel by Anthony Doerr · 880L

Unit Tasks

Gadgets and Glitches
pp. 66–77 · 5 Days

- Write an Argument
- Use Transitional Words and Phrases
- Present an Argument
- Reflect & Extend
  Write an Explanatory Essay
  Create a Business Plan
- Gadgets and Glitches Unit Test

Adapting Units of Instruction

Using the Planning Guides

What's the best approach to take when planning a unit?

Start with Your Learning Goals

Whether you are working with a curriculum map, pacing requirements, or other guidelines prescribed by your district, or are at liberty to develop your own curriculum, *Into Literature* has the resources you need to make effective teaching decisions.

● With your learning goals in mind, survey the standards included on the **Unit Planning Guide** and preview the cumulative activities on the **End-of-Unit Tasks Planning Guide.** Determine how you will assess student mastery: with a writing assignment, a project, a summative assessment, or a combination. Choose what to include in the unit based on what students will need to know to demonstrate mastery in these tasks.

Tips & Tricks!

Each **Unit Planning Guide** includes an asterisk next to skills that are covered on the **Unit Test**. If you choose to add or remove skills from your instruction, you may want to adjust the assessment accordingly. You can do this by editing the Word document and printing it out or using the custom assessment features on Ed and assigning the test digitally.

● Look closely at the **Unit Planning Guide** to get a sense of the texts, authors, genres, skills/standards, and suggested pacing for that unit.

● Preview the **Reader's Choice** options, including the Short Reads and Long Reads. Consider how you will incorporate independent reading in this unit. Think about additional titles you might like to recommend.

Using the Planning Guides

Plan for What You Need

Into Literature provides a number of pacing guidelines to help you plan.

How long should a unit take?

- Begin by reviewing the suggested pacing in the **Unit Planning Guide**. These are realistic estimates of how much time a lesson might take, but you are the best judge of the pacing for your students.

- There is more in-depth guidance on pacing in the **Lesson Planning Guide** pages, so spend a few minutes scanning each of the lessons.

Dark They Were, and Golden-Eyed
Science Fiction by Ray Bradbury

Close Read Screencast
Text Sketch ENG & SPANISH
Summary with Targeted Passages

pp. 212–237   **6** Days   540L

Analyze Science Fiction *   R
Analyze Mood *

Literary Analysis   W
Group Discussion
Podcast

Latin Roots *   V

Dangling Modifiers *   G

Selection Test   A

Plan

Dark They Were, and Golden-Eyed

Short Story by **Ray Bradbury,** pp. 212–237

Lesson Overview

 Suggested Pacing: 6 Days (50 minute classes)

Get Ready: 1 Day   **Read:** 3 Days   **Respond:** 2 Days

Day 1: paragraphs 1–77 | **Day 2:** paragraphs 78–246 | **Day 3:** paragraphs 247–278

- As you teach the lesson, look for embedded reminders of the pacing along the way, and a Quick Check formative assessment at the end of each day so you can monitor your students' understanding as you progress through the text.

WHOLE CLASS READING: **3 days**

Quick Check   Pacing DAY 1
Paragraphs 1–77

Use this quick activity to check students' understanding of the story so far.

- Display and read aloud these words: *frantic, excited, betrayed.*

  ...o consider Harry's actions so ...e their hands for the word they ...urately describes the mood the author is trying to establish.

What If My Students Don't Get It?

IF students don't choose "frantic," **THEN** highlight the moments Harry displays anxiety and discuss how those actions create the mood. (paragraphs 67 and 74)

Make the Unit Work for You

There are many adjustments you can make to each unit, and there are tips in the **Unit Planning Guide** to help you along.

What are some modifications I might make?

- Omit or swap out texts, based on student interest, time, or level of difficulty.

- "Upgrade" **Reader's Choice** selections as texts with instruction.

- Add your own texts or lessons into the mix, especially if you have personal favorites that match the theme or topic of the unit.

- Use a novel or Long Read as the anchor for a particular unit, supplementing it with the texts in the Student Edition.

- Change the skills/standards focus of a particular text, or cover even more skills and standards with the texts you are teaching. In many cases, the **Lesson Planning Guide** includes suggested alternate skills you might use.

- Choose a specific type of writing, media, or speaking and listening end-of-unit task, depending on what your students need more practice in or in preparation for a high-stakes assessment.

- *Ed* Give students more opportunities to apply key skills in the unit to fresh reads. You can do this by

  - choosing one of the Short Read or Long Read options suggested in the **Unit Planning Guide.**

  - visiting the **Text Library** on Ed and filtering by Lexile® or genre.

  - entering the skill as a search term on the platform and then using the component filter to select the **Leveled Text Library.**

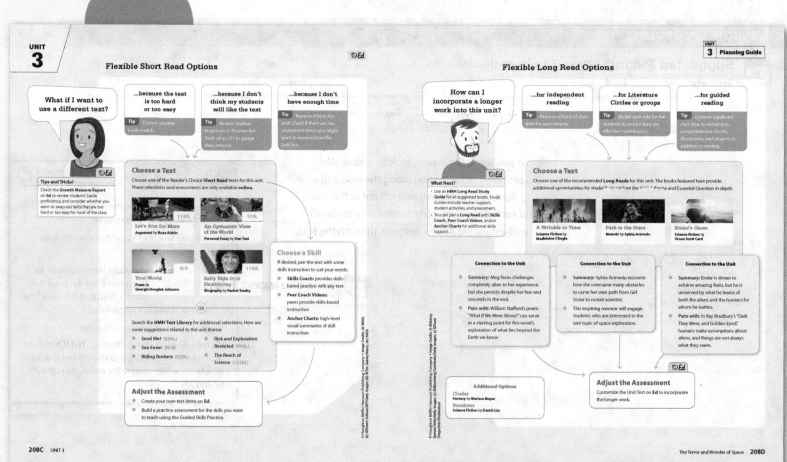

Customizing the Unit

What resources do you have that will help me make these changes?

Tips & Tricks!

For platform power users, you might consider using the available customization tools:
- Create custom lesson plans and build exactly the instruction you need.
- Start with *Into Literature* assessments. Edit them to suit your needs, adding your own items.

Featured Resource: Guided Skills Practice

Guided Skills Practice provides practice opportunities tied to particular skills. Each practice includes a leveled passage and a few related test items. A range of passages is available for each skill, so you can provide students with practice on that skill with a reading that is at *just* the right Lexile® level. For example:

Evaluate Author's Argument

- Some devices recognize your face. Is that a good thing? 700L
- Send Me! 800L
- Risk and Exploration Revisited 900L
- What Teenagers Need to Thrive 1000L
- Life in the Treetops 1100L

Find Flexible Options

Find the resources you need to meet your learning goals.

If you want to...	Try This!	Where?
Find different texts to include in the unit...	<ul><li>Leveled Texts across genres and at just the right Lexile® level</li><li>Printable Reader's Choice texts</li></ul>	**Text Library**
Incorporate a novel or other longer work...	<ul><li>Digital novels and nonfiction texts</li><li>HMH Study Guides and companion assessments</li></ul>	**Text Library**
Teach skills different from, or in addition to, those provided in the Student Edition...	<ul><li>Anchor Charts</li><li>Peer Coach Videos</li><li>Guided Skills Practice</li><li>Level Up Tutorials and Practice Tests</li><li>Skills Coach</li></ul>	**Intervention, Review, & Extension**
Provide extra practice opportunities for covered skills...	<ul><li>Interactive Writing, Grammar, Vocabulary, and Speaking & Listening Lessons</li><li>Guided Skills Practice</li><li>Level Up Tutorials and Practice Tests</li><li>Skills Coach</li></ul>	<ul><li>**Writing Resources**</li><li>**Grammar Resources**</li><li>**Vocabulary Resources**</li><li>**Speaking & Listening Resources**</li><li>**Intervention, Review, & Extension**</li></ul>
Use different cumulative tasks...	<ul><li>End-of-Unit Tasks and Reflect & Extend</li><li>Interactive Writing Lessons</li><li>Interactive Media Projects</li></ul>	<ul><li>**Teacher's Edition**</li><li>**Writing Resources**</li><li>**Media Projects**</li></ul>

Teaching with Novels and Longer Works

Understanding the Options

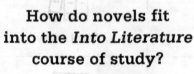

How do novels fit into the *Into Literature* course of study?

Tips & Tricks!

Find eBooks of classic novels in the **Digital Library** on Ed. These can be assigned to all your students.

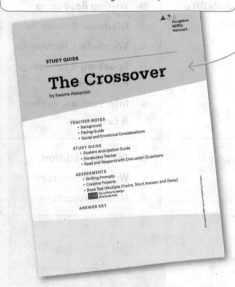

STUDY GUIDE

The Crossover
by Kwame Alexander

TEACHER NOTES
• Background
• Pacing Guide
• Social and Emotional Considerations

STUDY GUIDE
• Student Anticipation Guide
• Vocabulary Tracker
• Read and Respond with Discussion Questions

ASSESSMENTS
• Writing Prompts
• Creative Projects
• Book Test (Multiple Choice, Short Answer, and Essay)

ANSWER KEY

The Decision Is Up to You and Your Department

Whether you are looking for novels and other long reads that complement unit themes and skills or planning to incorporate titles you already teach regularly, *Into Literature* can support your practice. Take time to check out the resources that are available.

● Preview the **Suggested Long Reads** for each unit. The **Flexible Long Read Options** page in the Unit Planning Guide is the place to start. You'll find information about the three recommended titles that are featured in the Student Edition and supported with robust **Study Guides**, as well as about two additional recommended titles supported by a modified Study Guide. All Study Guides can be found online.

● Familiarize yourself with the **Study Guides**. They include teacher notes, a vocabulary tracker, analysis questions, writing prompts, assessments, and other support for previewing the book and teaching it in a variety of ways.

● **Ed** Gather support for any additional titles you want to bring in. This might include **Peer Coach** and **Skills Coach** for the reinforcement of relevant skills, **Notice & Note writing frames** and **bookmarks**, and **interactive graphic organizers**.

● Make some choices. Each unit includes more texts than you can cover in a six- or eight-week course of study, especially when factoring in the suggested Long Reads and Reader's Choice selections. You have to decide what to use, and how. Will you teach a novel as a whole-class project, offer several novels to choose from for Literature Circles, assign students independent reading, or some combination throughout the year?

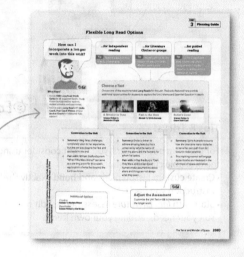

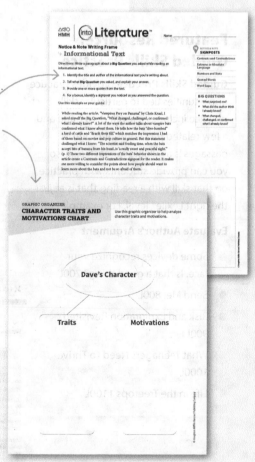

Choosing Your Approach

How can I implement a successful whole-class long read?

Ⓔd

Tips & Tricks!

The **Notice & Note Chart** on pages T30–T32 of the Teacher's Edition includes examples of each signpost drawn from recommended long read titles. If you expect students to use signposts, consider using one of these examples to model how.

Create an Experience That Brings the Class Together

Whole-class reads allow you to create exposure to important books and model best practices for analyzing long works. Many teachers assign a whole-class read in the first part of the school year and then allow students more choice in later grading periods. Others may only have time to teach one novel a year and choose a whole-class experience that everyone can share.

Since so many students will be spending so much time on it, take care to choose a worthy title with wide appeal. The Teacher's Notes in the **Study Guide** can help you.

- Read about the author and, where relevant, critical perspectives.
- Preview key themes and literary elements.
- Scan the **Social and Emotional Considerations** section in the Teacher's Notes, which can help you anticipate whether a book is likely to meet your community's standards and whether you may want to communicate with parents and guardians before reading.

Sensitive Content	Context	Evaluating the Outcome
Death of the main characters' father	Mr. Bell's illness and death are central to the story's plot. The father suffers numerous ominous symptoms of heart disease and refuses to take actions to improve his health.	The tragic loss of their father results in the twins' reaching out to each other and ending their conflict. The kind words and actions of others comfort Josh and show how loved his father was. **Ask:** What positive lessons might Josh gain from his father's death? What struggles will he face because of it?
Sexist views of girls	Josh begins by focusing on the appearances of Alexis, who begins dating JB, and his friend Vondie's girlfriend, who is not named.	Josh eventually develops a fuller view of the girls' personalities. **Ask:** Why do you think the author chose to describe the girls this way? Does the outcome make up for the initial descriptions?
Father stopped for a questionable traffic violation	On the way to an important game, Dad is stopped for having a broken taillight. He has accidentally left his driver's license at home but explains who he is. The officer requests his autograph and lets him go.	Unlike many recent events that ended badly because of racial bias, in this case Dad's status as a sports star prevents a negative outcome. **Ask:** How might the traffic stop have turned out differently? How do you feel about the outcome in the book?
Family estrangement	The coach shares what he learned from losing his relationship with his brother to help Josh and JB avoid the same negative outcome.	Josh and JB eventually reconcile. **Ask:** Where would you draw the line between a minor conflict with a family member and an unforgivable act? What do you think of the choices the characters make?
Divorce	It's mentioned in passing that Alexis's parents are divorced.	Alexis has adapted to her split living arrangement and seems comfortable with it. **Ask:** What is a major change that you or a friend was unhappy about but eventually adapted to? What strategies made this adaptation possible?

How do I make Literature Circles work in my classroom?

Allow Choice and Set Expectations

Many teachers find that allowing students some choice increases their motivation and focus. Literature Circles or book groups are a good way to do this, as long as you provide enough structure.

- Use the **Suggested Long Reads** and/or other books available to you to create a list for students to choose from. Ask students to pick a first and second choice so that you have some options for balancing groups. As much as possible, form groups based on book choice, not ability.

- Assign students jobs that cater to their specific skills, drawn from the roles shown below. Allow students to switch roles as they wish, emphasizing student choice.

Leader   Note Taker   Time Keeper   Participation Tracker

- Tell group members to develop a reading schedule. They should think through pacing and homework load.

- Have students take notes during their discussions or fill out a text-agnostic graphic organizer, but do not create a text-specific assignment for them to complete. Their own insights and questions should drive each of their discussions.

Socratic Seminars

Consider having groups conduct a Socratic Seminar.

- Students create open-ended questions to ask each other during a formal discussion.

- The seminar should be student-led with little involvement from the teacher.

- Students' questions should build on each other's ideas and demonstrate their understanding of the text read.

- All students should participate. Evaluate their responses based on the insight and examples they provide.

How can I monitor students' independent reading?

Introduce Strategies and Let Students Do the Work

Providing students a chance to explore their own reading interests can engage them and encourage independence. Here are some suggestions for creating accountability.

- Meet with each student for a booktalk. Students should be prepared to talk about the main conflicts or ideas in the book, and give their opinions of them.

- Have students track and analyze **Notice & Note** signposts they identify while reading. They can use the **Notice & Note** Writing Frames to do so, or create a two-column chart with the signposts listed in one column and the examples and analysis in the other.

- Ask students to create dialectical journals. Have students identify significant quotations from the text in one column. In a second column, have students describe each quote's significance. Did it reveal something about the character or events? Did it impact the student's reading in some way?

Tips & Tricks!

Steer advanced learners toward higher Lexile® texts and challenge them to seek out and analyze competing critical perspectives.

Assessing Long Reads

> How can I integrate skills/standards instruction with long reads?

Identify the Skills You Want to Reinforce

- If you're working with **Recommended Long Reads**, the **Study Guides** will include a list of skills that you can match with your standards. Otherwise, preview the text on your own.

- Consider teaching the core standards with the **Analyze & Apply** or **Collaborate & Compare** lessons in each unit. Then have students apply those skills and standards in their Literature Circles or in their independent reading of Long Reads.

- Reinforce the skills you want to teach with text-agnostic resources such as **Peer Coach**, **Skills Coach**, and graphic organizers that can be used across Literature Circles. Emphasize the skills you want the class to focus on by displaying anchor charts.

Choose and Customize

Use a combination of standardized assessment, writing-based assessment, and projects to understand what students have learned from their reading. *Into Literature* provides a variety of options depending on how closely you've woven the Long Reads into the unit themes and standards and whether you've used a **Recommended Long Read**.

> How can I assess what students have learned?

Tips & Tricks!

The **Media Projects** on Ed can often be adapted to work with a Long Read, providing an additional opportunity for students to demonstrate how the novel relates to the unit's Essential Question.

- If you used the Long Read to connect to unit topic and themes, choose an end-of-unit task. The writing and speaking and listening opportunities allow students to demonstrate their understanding of how the book relates to the Essential Question. You can adapt the prompt to suit your needs.

- If you used the Long Reads to teach or reinforce the unit standards, customize the **Unit Tests** available on the platform. These are aligned to the reading, language, and vocabulary skills taught throughout the unit, and can be customized to eliminate any skills you haven't covered.

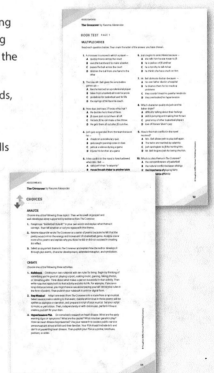

- If students read a Recommended Long Read, use the **Book Test** in the Study Guide, which is printable and available to assign on Ed. Use the Writing Prompts and Creative Projects available in the **Choices** section of the Study Guide. You can also assign the Extension activities on the **Reader's Choice** page of the Student Edition.

- If you've brought in an additional novel and taught it as a stand-alone unit, you may want to peruse the Writing Prompts and Creative Projects in the **Study Guides** to find assignments you can adapt to fit your purposes.

Program Guide 51

Student Engagement

Igniting Student Engagement

Knowing Your Audience

Remember—It's All About Them

Getting your students excited about reading literature starts with developing a deeper understanding of their interests.

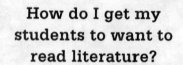

- At the beginning of the year, use an Interest Inventory to gain insights into students' favorite genres. Write a list of genres on a flip chart on the wall. Have students mark their three favorite genres in order of preference. Discuss their choices as a class. Another way to gauge students' preferences is to use polling software to create a survey. Use this information to select the texts you teach or recommend for independent reading.

- Before you start a new unit, use the **Spark Your Learning** feature—specifically, **Preview the Texts**—to see which titles generate the most interest and excitement. Review the titles, genres, and teasers as a class. Use a show of hands to see which title is most or least appealing. If you have flexibility in the texts you teach, or the order of those texts, use this insight to drive your planning.

- Use the **Collaborate & Compare** feature in each unit to increase student engagement. Comparing classic and contemporary connections, different points of view, or various text formats can add interest and relevance to instruction.

Sparking Their Learning

Make the Connection

Into Literature was built with this question in mind. At the beginning of each unit and lesson, you will find a variety of options for hooking students and getting them invested in the learning. Try these suggestions:

> How do I ignite my students' interest in the topic or text that I'm about to teach?

- As a start to each unit, divide the class into small groups and prompt groups to discuss the opening illustration, along with the Analyze the Image question. Have each group share its ideas with the class.

- *Ed* Play the **Stream to Start Video**, available in the **Student eBook**, to build students' knowledge about the unit topic.

- Use the activities in the **Spark Your Learning** feature at the beginning of the unit to brainstorm connections to pop culture and to get students thinking about the Essential Question. Consult the notes in your Teacher's Edition for flexible grouping ideas.

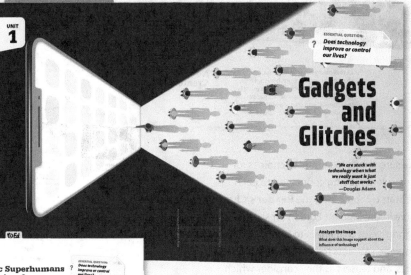

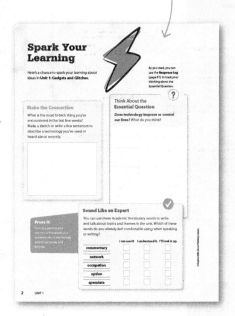

- *Ed* Browse for connections to current events on the **HMH Current Events** site, which is updated frequently.

- Launch each lesson in the unit with the **Engage Your Brain** activities, which are designed to get students sketching, quick-writing, and discussing key ideas related to the text.

> How can I give my students choices, yet still accomplish my learning goals?

Decide Which Kinds of Choice to Offer

Even if you are unable to let students' interests and choices dictate the texts you teach, you can still empower them with other kinds of choices. Here are some options:

● Have the class, small groups, or individuals select from the **Choices** activities at the end of each lesson.

● Invite students to choose how they will demonstrate their understanding of what they've learned in each unit. The writing and speaking and listening tasks are options, of course. Discover additional options in the **Reflect & Extend** feature at the end of each unit. One of those options is a **Media Project**, which is a great way to try out project-based learning in your classroom.

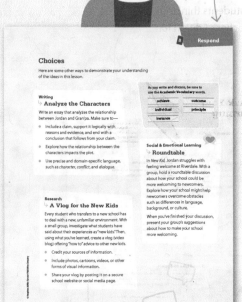

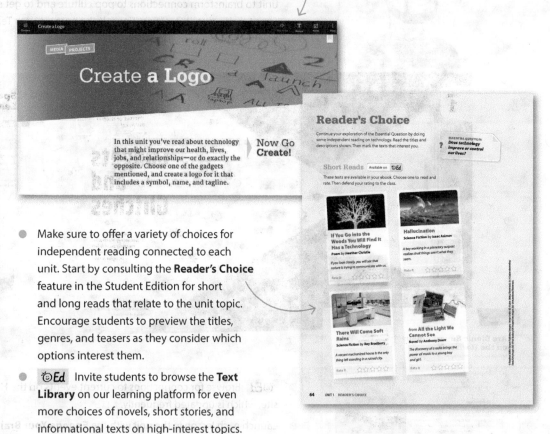

● Make sure to offer a variety of choices for independent reading connected to each unit. Start by consulting the **Reader's Choice** feature in the Student Edition for short and long reads that relate to the unit topic. Encourage students to preview the titles, genres, and teasers as they consider which options interest them.

● **Ed** Invite students to browse the **Text Library** on our learning platform for even more choices of novels, short stories, and informational texts on high-interest topics.

Going Beyond the Book Report

What are some high-interest ways for students to demonstrate what they learned in their independent reading?

Tips & Tricks!

Make sure that students explain and reflect on their finished products. This step is just as important as the project itself!

Build in Creativity and Variety

Book reports are relics of the past. Today, there are countless creative ways—and digital tools—to help students share their independent reading with their class, their community, and the world. Such projects can tap into students' creativity and digital expertise, while increasing engagement along the way.

The **Reader's Choice** feature in each unit offers a variety of project ideas that you may want to explore. Here are a few ideas that can work equally well whether students are reading short texts, novels, or longer works of nonfiction.

Project Ideas:

Produce a Book Talk
A book talk is a short presentation about a book that persuades others to read it. Highlight aspects of the book that will intrigue potential readers.

Write a Text-Message Exchange
Create text messages between two characters, using knowledge of their motivations, ways of communicating, personalities, and relationships.

Spot Notice & Note Signposts
Find three Notice & Note signposts in a text. Use the **Writing Frames** online to go from identification to analysis and evaluation in writing.

Design a Social Media Profile
Create a social-media profile page for a character in a story. Include images, status updates, and comments that reflect that character's traits.

Create a Graphic Novel
Illustrate a key scene or event in a novel or short story.

Draft a Movie Script
Write a script that adapts a scene or event from a text. Consider how camera shots, sound effects, and music enhance the story.

Design a Book Jacket
Create a book jacket for a text, relying on layout, color, and text to communicate a mood or a theme. Include a summary or teaser that will make people want to buy the book!

Craft a Haiku
Write a haiku—an unrhymed poem of three lines of 5, 7, and 5 syllables each—that communicates something about a character, event, or theme of a text.

Draw a Sketchnote
A sketchnote is a form of visual note-taking that captures a text's main ideas in words and doodles. Create a sketchnote to remember key takeaways from any informational text or the plot of a fictional work.

Tweet It
Try the 280-character challenge! Craft a tweet that summarizes a key idea or theme of a text.

Create a Word Cloud
Record a cloud of words from a memoir or nonfiction narrative, with the title of the text in the center. Explain how the chosen words reflect the author's tone.

Produce a Podcast
Record a podcast discussion with two other classmates who read the same text. Share opinions of the text and the characters.

Integrating Social & Emotional Learning

Understanding the Competencies

> What is social and emotional learning (SEL)?

 ### Social & Emotional Learning

Social and Emotional Learning is the process by which people develop the ability to understand and manage emotions, set and achieve positive goals, feel and show empathy for others, establish and maintain positive relationships, and make responsible decisions.

Into Literature focuses on the core competencies of social and emotional learning developed by the Collaborative for Academic, Social, and Emotional Learning (CASEL).

SELF-AWARENESS

The ability to accurately recognize one's own emotions, thoughts, and values and how they influence behavior. The ability to accurately assess one's strengths and limitations, with a well-grounded sense of confidence, optimism, and a "growth mindset."

- Identifying Emotions
- Accurate Self- Perception
- Recognizing Strengths
- Self-Confidence
- Self-Efficacy

SELF-MANAGEMENT

The ability to successfully regulate one's emotions, thoughts, and behaviors in different situations—effectively managing stress, controlling impulses, and motivating oneself. The ability to set and work toward personal and academic goals.

- Impulse Control
- Stress Management
- Self-Discipline
- Self-Motivation
- Goal Setting
- Organizational Skills

SOCIAL AWARENESS

The ability to take the perspective of and empathize with others, including those from diverse backgrounds and cultures. The ability to understand social and ethical norms for behavior and to recognize family, school, and community resources and supports.

- Perspective-Taking
- Empathy
- Appreciating Diversity
- Respect for Others

RESPONSIBLE DECISION-MAKING

The ability to make constructive choices about personal behavior and social interactions based on ethical standards, safety concerns, and social norms. The realistic evaluation of consequences of various actions, and a consideration of the well-being of oneself and others.

- Identifying Problems
- Analyzing Situations
- Solving Problems
- Evaluating
- Reflecting
- Ethical Responsibility

RELATIONSHIP SKILLS

The ability to establish and maintain healthy and rewarding relationships with diverse individuals and groups. The ability to communicate clearly, listen well, cooperate with others, resist inappropriate social pressure, negotiate conflict constructively, and seek and offer help when needed.

- Communication
- Social Engagement
- Relationship Building
- Teamwork

Diagram labels: HOMES & COMMUNITIES · SCHOOLS · CLASSROOMS · SELF-AWARENESS · SELF-MANAGEMENT · SOCIAL & EMOTIONAL LEARNING · RESPONSIBLE DECISION-MAKING · SOCIAL AWARENESS · RELATIONSHIP SKILLS · SEL CURRICULUM & INSTRUCTION · SCHOOLWIDE PRACTICES & POLICIES · FAMILY & COMMUNITY PARTNERSHIPS · © 2017 CASEL. ALL RIGHTS RESERVED

Getting Started

Why does SEL matter?

It Helps Students Succeed

As an educator, you know that learning goes beyond acquiring facts and expanding knowledge. It's a personal journey that requires curiosity, perseverance, and growth. When students are taught the competencies and given opportunities to practice, they'll be better able to cope with the highs and lows of school and the learning process itself. Benefits include:

- Improved quality of teacher-student interactions
- Improved student performance
- Ease of social adjustments for students
- Increase in positive behaviors that result in positive outcomes
- Increase in supportive classroom culture

Start with Direct Instruction

Research shows that direct instruction in Social and Emotional Learning is effective. Make students aware of the concept early in the year.

- Start with a whole-class reading of **"The Most Important Subject Is You"** by Carol Jago, which appears on pages FM28–FM31 of the Student Edition.
- Consider using the content of the essay as a jumping-off point for a class discussion about how to foster a collaborative, supportive learning environment. Create anchor charts or other visual reminders of the key principles that emerge, such as having respectful conversations, valuing individual voices, managing emotions, and building relationships.

How and when do I introduce my students to SEL?

- Decide whether you want to introduce your students to the specific language of the competencies. These labels do not appear in the Student Edition, but the Teacher's Edition provides language to share with students at point of use as you see fit.

Integrating SEL into the Curriculum

How can I connect SEL with my teaching of literature?

Use Unit Topics and Texts to Reinforce the Concepts

Research suggests that integrating SEL directly into the core curriculum is an effective practice. You can use the unit topics and selections to reinforce instruction of SEL concepts, and you can use SEL concepts to encourage students to analyze the selections through a different lens. *Into Literature* provides options for both, and plenty of opportunities for students to practice.

- In the **Introduce the Unit** feature, a Teacher's Edition note supports direct instruction in a specific competency.

- In the **Choices** section of every lesson, there's an activity in the Student Edition or the Teacher's Edition that connects the content of the literature to a competency.

Social & Emotional Learning

Relationship Skills Space exploration requires the collaboration of hundreds or even thousands of people working in teams. Brainstorm with students a list of relationship skills that help teams function effectively. Then, tell students that they will work in groups to come up with a public relations strategy to promote a new NASA mission to Mars. After they have finished, ask students to evaluate the teamwork of their group. How well did group members listen as others shared ideas? Were there any disagreements? If so, how were they resolved? What changes could have improved the group's teamwork?

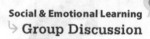

Social & Emotional Learning
↳ **Group Discussion**

For much of the story, Harry Bittering is the only one who resists the physical and cultural changes occurring among the settlers. In a small group, discuss the following questions about the peer pressure Harry experiences in the story.

- Is it spoken pressure, unspoken, or both?

- Do the other settlers influence Harry through positive emotions (such as showing their own happiness) or negative emotions (such as making fun of him)?

- Why does Harry ultimately accept the viewpoint of the other settlers? Was this the right decision?

Dark They Were, and Golden-Eyed **235**

- In the **Reflect & Extend** section at the end of every unit, an SEL note in the Teacher's Edition provides guidance for incorporating an SEL competency into one of the activities.

- In the **Lesson Planning Guide**, every lesson that has an **SEL Choices** activity notes the SEL competency associated with it, so you can plan ahead. Selections that include especially sensitive content will have an additional note to provide you with suggestions and strategies for dealing with issues related to the text.

- The **Spark Your Learning** activities that open each unit and the **Engage Your Brain** activities that open each lesson provide opportunities for students to practice self-awareness, social awareness, and relationship skills.

- Text-based questions and writing activities encourage students to consider the factors and consequences involved in characters' decision-making, thus strengthening their own decision-making abilities.

 Social & Emotional Learning

Reflect on the Essential Question Help students develop **self-awareness** by answering the questions and completing the sentence stems independently. Then have students pair off and interview each other about their responses.

- Circulate during these interviews to get a sense of students' thoughts.

- Wrap up with a whole-class discussion in which you reinforce key themes from the interviews.

- If you observe any consistent challenges that students encountered during the unit, have them share strategies for overcoming them.

Providing Ongoing Support

What support is there for me as I navigate difficult topics and texts with my students?

Preview and Communicate

Texts that allow students to develop empathy, contemplate life's challenges, and prepare for tough decisions can include sensitive material. It's not always possible to know what topics and content will provoke controversy or trigger trauma-based responses among individuals or groups. You know your students and communities best, so *Into Literature* provides you with ways to preview materials and adjust and prepare as you see fit. When students, parents, and guardians are informed about what the curriculum will include and why, they are more likely to respond positively.

- ⊙Ed The **Build Family Engagement** note in the Teacher's Edition Unit Opener refers to an editable letter that can be sent to students' homes, providing an opportunity to preview and explain any potentially sensitive material that will be covered. You can find the letter on Ed, the learning platform.

- The **What Is This Story About?** note in each Teacher's Edition **Lesson Planning Guide** summarizes the selection so that you will be aware of the topics covered.

⊙Ed
Editable Letter to Families

Build Family Engagement

Involve students' families in their learning by sending home an email or letter introducing Unit 3. Use the editable letter provided online or write your own. You might include

- **Unit 3 Theme:** In "The Terror and Wonder of Space," students will consider what it might be like to explore space and reflect on the hazards and limits of exploration.

- **Essential Question:** Suggest that students continue the discussion at home with parents or caregivers as they read each text.

- **List of Texts:** Use the Preview the Texts feature on page 211 to gather the titles, genres, and previews of each text students will read.

- **Reader's Choice:** Use the brief descriptions of the Short Reads and Longs Reads provided on pages 298–299 to inform parents and caregivers of students' choices.

- **Unit Tasks:** Explain that students will conclude the unit by writing an argument taking a stance on space travel. They will also plan and create a podcast explaining how a spacewalk is accomplished.

What Is This Story About?

The Bittering family arrives on Mars as part of a small colony. Within moments of their arrival, Mr. Bittering becomes obsessed by the idea of returning to Earth. He senses that he will be changed in some way and becomes fearful of losing his identity. Mr. Bittering begins building a rocket in order to return to Earth.

In time, he notices slight but significant changes in his family. Gradually, all of the colonists attain Martian characteristics and begin to use the Martian language. Finally, the Bittering family is transformed into a Martian family. Another rocket arrives on Mars and finds no Earthlings.

⊙Ed
Summaries in Other Languages

STUDENT ANTICIPATION GUIDE

Before Reading Before reading the book, mark your response to each item below in the "Before" column:

- Mark a plus sign (+) if you agree.
- Mark a minus sign (–) if you disagree.
- Mark a question mark (?) if you are unsure of your opinion.

Then freewrite about one of the items.

	BEFORE	AFTER
1. People should be punished when they do something wrong.		
2. Choices about how we live our own lives are our own business.		
3. Someone's first loyalty should be to his or her family.		
4. Things that seem risky should be avoided.		
5. If you get into trouble for helping someone, then they owe you.		

After Reading When you have finished reading and discussing the book, mark your responses to the items above in the "After" column. Then freewrite about one item. You may choose to write about

- the same item you chose for your Before Reading freewriting
- an item about which your opinion changed
- an item about which your opinion grew much stronger

- In the **HMH Study Guides,** a **Social and Emotional Considerations** section provides a chart showing potential triggering issues, and an **Anticipation Guide** prompts students to preview emotionally-charged elements of the text ahead of time to help prepare them.

How can my school extend social and emotional learning beyond the *Into Literature* curriculum?

Try a Community Read with *A Chance in the World*

Social and emotional learning is especially effective when a whole school or whole grade commits to the process. HMH has partnered with author, speaker, and executive Steve Pemberton to create an SEL-focused curriculum around his inspirational memoir *A Chance in the World*. It's designed to engage students and bring communities together while fostering awareness of and growth in the CASEL core competencies.

The curriculum is appropriate for grades 8–12 and is built to be flexible. It can be used as

- an all-school read, with all students, teachers, and staff participating
- a summer read, which may include community library participation
- an all-grade read, perhaps for incoming or outgoing classes
- a core text in an ELA class, utilizing the optional academic component of the curriculum

READY TO TAKE A CHANCE?

Curriculum Guide
A Community Reading Experience

A CHANCE IN THE WORLD

"We aren't measured by what happens to us but rather by how we respond to it."
—Steve Pemberton, author of "A Chance in the World"

NOW A MAJOR MOTION PICTURE

USA TODAY Bestseller
Revised *and* Updated

A
CHANCE
IN THE
WORLD

*An Orphan Boy,
a Mysterious Past,
and How
He Found a Place
Called Home*

STEVE
PEMBERTON

Providing Ongoing Support

Why this text?

It Engages Students and Explores Important Themes

A Chance in the World is a story of resilience, portraying Steve Pemberton's terrifying experiences in the foster-care system and his quest to uncover the truth about his origins. The memoir shines a harsh light on society's failure to protect vulnerable youths. Yet it also shows how acts of kindness can profoundly affect lives, and that we all have the potential to overcome adversity.

The book has moved and motivated many adolescents who see their own lives reflected in aspects of the author's experience. It encourages reflection on important questions: Where do I belong? How can I succeed when others dismiss my worth? How can I help those who need it?

What does the curriculum include?

Social & Emotional Learning Resources and More

The **Curriculum Guide** was developed with input from educators who have successfully used *A Chance in the World* in their schools. The resources in it are also available digitally and supplemented by select digital-only assets. There are three sections.

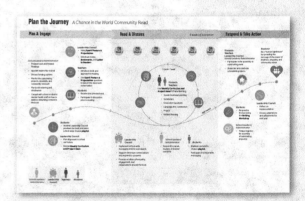

- **Plan & Engage** includes an experience map to help plan the journey, a letter to readers from Steve Pemberton, posters to generate excitement, and more.

- **Read & Discuss** divides the book into six parts. Each part contains a social and emotional learning activity, vocabulary, discussion questions, English language arts connections, suggested project ideas, and connections to related readings across multiple genres, which are included.

- **Respond & Take Action** includes culminating projects and an in-depth writing workshop on personal narrative.

Close Reading & Analysis

Using Notice & Note for Close Reading

Getting Started

What is Notice & Note, and what are signposts?

ⓝ NOTICE & NOTE

Notice & Note is a close-reading protocol grounded in the research of Dr. Kylene Beers and Dr. Robert E. Probst and designed to encourage students to be active readers. At the heart of Notice & Note are signposts—key aspects of literary and informational texts that are worth paying attention to. Each signpost is associated with an anchor question.

Kylene and Bob developed Notice & Note after studying the books most commonly taught in middle and high school. As they read, they noticed regularly-occurring features that helped them better understand key elements such as character development, internal conflict, and theme. They established three criteria that each feature had to meet in order to be taught to students:

1. It had to have a characteristic that made it noticeable, so that it could be identified.

2. It had to show up in a majority of works.

3. It had to help readers who noticed it understand something about their own responses or interpretations.

In response to student and teacher feedback, Kylene and Bob streamlined the signposts and anchor questions. Once they did, they noticed students adopting them more quickly, as well as generating more of their own questions—the ultimate goal. They later expanded into informational texts with similarly positive results.

Preview the Signposts

The chart you'll see when you turn the page includes the six literary signposts and five informational text signposts, plus the Big Questions that are important to ask when reading nonfiction.

How will Notice & Note help my students?

Draw Students Deep Into the Text

When students are taught to look for signposts and ask the anchor questions, they begin to read more thoughtfully. Through initial modeling and prompting, and then with increasing independence, students will make predictions and inferences based on text evidence and connect what they read with their own lives and the world around them.

Teachers report that signposts create rich fodder for conversation. Students of all levels can share the signposts they find in a text and debate their meaning, building on each other's ideas and sharing evidence that supports their interpretations. Instead of waiting for a teacher to guide them through the text, students begin to make their own meaning.

Learning by Example

The excerpts below are from the story "Thank You, M'am" by Langston Hughes. They contain several **Contrasts and Contradictions**, which are the most commonly-found signpost. The anchor question is "Why would the character act (or feel) this way?"

The annotations show a summarized version of how a teacher might work through a lesson after having introduced the signpost.

In the story, the boy has just tried to steal the woman's purse, and she's grabbed him.

"If I turn you loose, will you run?" asked the woman.

"Yes'm," said the boy.

"Then I won't turn you loose," said the woman. She did not release him.

"I'm very sorry, lady, I'm sorry," whispered the boy.

"Um-hum! And your face is dirty. I got a great mind to wash your face for you. Ain't you got nobody home to tell you to wash your face?"

"No'm," said the boy.

CC "Then it will get washed this evening," said the large woman starting up the street, dragging the frightened boy behind her.

MODEL

Here I pause and tell students the woman is acting in a way that contrasts with what I'd expect. If someone were trying to steal from me, I wouldn't invite them home to wash their face! So I'm going to ask why she would act that way. Is she feeling sorry for him? I'll have to keep reading to find out.

---

up the street. When she got to her door, she dragged the boy inside, down a hall, and into a large kitchenette-furnished room at the rear of the house. She switched on the light and left the door open. The boy could hear other roomers laughing and talking in the large house. Some of their doors were open, too, so he knew he and the woman were not alone. The woman still had him by the neck in the middle of her room.

She said, "What is your name?"

"Roger," answered the boy.

"Then, Roger, you go to that sink and wash your face," said the woman, whereupon she turned him loose—at last. Roger **CC** looked at the door—looked at the woman—looked at the door—*and went to the sink.*

GUIDE

I tell students the contrast I noticed: Roger had been trying to get away, but now that he has the chance, he decides to stay. This time I ask students to pose the anchor question, and have them break into pairs for a minute or so to answer it. Students might offer a variety of reasons why he acts this way. I tell them that as we continue reading, they should mark a small CC next to any Contrasts and Contradictions they notice.

CC When they were finished eating she got up and said, "Now, here, take this ten dollars and buy yourself some blue suede shoes. And next time, do not make the mistake of **latching** onto *my* pocketbook *nor nobody else's*—because shoes come by devilish like that will burn your feet. I got to get my rest now. But I wish you would behave yourself, son, from here on in."

RELEASE

I invite students to share the most interesting CCs they noticed and share what they think about them. This usually leads to a rich conversation, as students dig into the characters' motivations and developments.

Close Reading & Analysis

CONTRASTS & CONTRADICTIONS

A sharp contrast between what we would expect and what we observe the character doing; behavior that contradicts previous behavior or well-established patterns

Why would the character act (feel) this way?

AHA MOMENT

A sudden realization of something that shifts a character's actions or understanding of self, others, or the world

How might this change things?

TOUGH QUESTIONS

Questions characters raise that reveal their inner struggles

What does this question make me wonder about?

WORDS OF THE WISER

The advice or insight about life that a wiser character, who is usually older, offers to the main character

What is the life lesson, and how might this affect the character?

AGAIN & AGAIN

Events, images, or particular words that recur over a portion of the story

Why might the author bring this up again and again?

MEMORY MOMENT

A recollection by a character that interrupts the forward progress of the story

Why might this memory moment be important?

Signposts for Informational Texts

BIG QUESTIONS

It's important to take a **Questioning Stance** or attitude when you read nonfiction.

• *What surprised me?*
• *What did the author think I already knew?*
• *What challenged, changed, or confirmed what I already knew?*

CONTRASTS & CONTRADICTIONS

A sharp contrast between what we would expect and what we observe happening; a difference between two or more elements in the texts

What is the difference and why does it matter?

EXTREME OR ABSOLUTE LANGUAGE

Language that leaves no doubt about a situation or an event, allows no compromise, or seems to exaggerate or overstate a case

Why did the author use this language?

QUOTED WORDS

Opinions or conclusions of someone who is an expert on the subject or someone who might be a participant in or a witness to an event; or the author might cite other people to provide support for a point

Why was this person quoted or cited, and what did this add?

NUMBERS AND STATS

Specific quantities or comparisons to depict the amount, size, or scale; or the writer is vague when we would expect more precision

Why did the author use these numbers or amounts?

WORD GAPS

Vocabulary that is unfamiliar to the reader—for example, a word with multiple meanings, a rare or technical word, or one with a far-removed antecedent

Do I know this word from someplace else? Can I find clues in the sentence to help me understand the word?

Introducing Students to Notice & Note

How do I introduce the signposts to my students?

Start with the Signposts

There's no one right way to introduce the signposts. Here are some tips to guide you.

- Start by having the whole class read and discuss the **essay** on pages FM22–FM25 of the Student Edition.

- Reserve time at the beginning of the school year to acquaint students with the signposts. Start by focusing on just one or two at a time.

- Consider the order. The signposts appear in the chart in order of the frequency with which they occur. Many teachers start with Contrasts and Contradictions, because selections often contain several of these. However, you may want to let the selection you're using drive the order. The **Lesson Overview** in the Teacher's Edition for each selection will tell you which signposts are covered.

- Consider using short film or television clips to introduce each signpost. On pages T30–T32, your Teacher's Edition suggests media examples that have worked for others.

- Connect with Kylene and Bob, as well as other devoted followers of Notice & Note, on social media. Find inspiring ideas and answers to common questions.

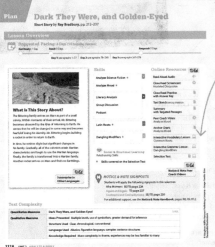

Connect to Curriculum

The "stickiness" of the signpost names can help students remember them. Yet, it helps to reinforce the direct connections between signposts and the academic language of literature. *Aha moment* is an epiphany; *again and again* is repetition.

Here are some ideas for making this connection:

- Point out the *Literary Analysis Connection* notes in the Student Edition Notice & Note handbook on pages R8–R13.

- Use the skills listed in the handbook to create a crosswalk between your standards and the signposts. This is a great way to reinforce Notice & Note within your ELA professional learning community.

How can I connect Notice & Note to skills and standards?

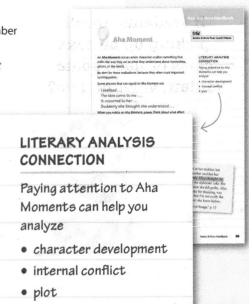

LITERARY ANALYSIS CONNECTION

Paying attention to Aha Moments can help you analyze

- character development
- internal conflict
- plot

After I teach a signpost, will students really be able to spot it on their own?

Ed

Tips & Tricks!

An expanded version of the chart appears on Student Edition pages FM26–FM27 and on Ed. Some teachers print and laminate the chart to use throughout the year during small-group work.

Reinforce and Practice with Signposts

Identifying signposts takes continued practice. Visual reminders help too. Here are some tips for keeping Notice & Note fresh in your students' minds.

- Display Notice & Note **Anchor Charts** describing each signpost on the wall.

- Print and distribute the bookmarks with descriptions of each signpost. Challenge students to use the Notice & Note annotation marks to identify signposts in their independent reading.

- Use the **Lesson Overview** in the Teacher's Edition to stay alert to opportunities to reinforce signposts within a lesson. As a bellringer activity, have students review the **Notice & Note handbook** page for any signposts you'll be discussing in that day's lesson.

- Use the questions in the side margins of the Student Edition to model and guide close reading using signposts.

Memory Moment

A recollection by a character that interrupts the forward progress of the story.

Text Clues
- A character has a flashback that interrupts the present.
- "I suddenly remembered. . ." or "Thinking back. . ."
- A character tells an old story from the past.

Ask Yourself

Why might this memory be important?

The answer to this question can tell you more about a **character** or a possible **theme**, or it can foreshadow what's to come later in the **plot**.

---

on the table. Rich, white chocolate piping swirled over dark mocha. Ornate candy violets decorated the cake's tall sides.

"Awesome, Mom," said Alice. She couldn't remember her mother ever making a homemade cake before. "You blow first," she said to Jenny as she sat down. "You're the oldest."

"By two minutes," said Jenny, "and anyway, maybe I'm not the oldest anymore."

"What do you mean?"

"You might be older than me now with your new body. You might be old enough to drive for all we know."

Alice's brown eyes widened. "Mom, if my body is sixteen, does that mean I can get my license?"

"Forget it," her mother said as she lit the cake. "You could barely walk six months ago." She switched out the lights.

N NOTICE & NOTE
MEMORY MOMENT

When you notice the narrator has interrupted the forward progress of a story by bringing up something from the past, you've found a **Memory Moment** signpost.

Notice & Note: Review what happens in paragraphs 49–52, and mark any details about what happened in the past.

Compare: Why might this memory be important?

If students aren't picking up on text clues or need some review, what do I do?

Review the Signposts

It won't be long before your students are surprising you with all the signposts they discover in their reading. Every once in a while, though, it may help to review strategies for finding signposts. Here's how:

- Have students review the **Notice & Note Peer Coach videos** for the signposts they struggle with, or play them as a refresher for the whole class before a relevant lesson.

- Review with students the signposts and examples in the Student Edition **Notice & Note handbook**.

Aha Moment
A sudden realization of something that shifts a character's actions or understanding of self, others, or the world

AHA! I GET IT NOW!

Extending & Enriching

How do I use Notice & Note with novels and long reads?

Scaffold and Release

Whether read by the whole class, as part of book groups, or independently, novels and memoirs are ideal texts in which to notice signposts, because they they include deep character development and long story arcs with multiple themes.

- If possible, model the discovery of a signpost in a novel before asking students to do so in groups or on their own. The chart on **Teacher's Edition** pages T30–T32 provides examples from Recommended Long Reads with which to model each signpost.

- Have students share the signposts they find with a small group or the class. Make sure they answer the anchor questions as part of their analysis.

- 😊 *Ed* Print and distribute the **Notice & Note Writing Frames** online. Prompt students to choose one signpost to focus on and analyze for other readers of the text. Challenge students to use the academic language of literature in their response.

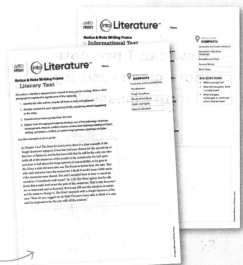

Is Notice & Note appropriate for advanced readers?

Apply to Complex Text

Notice & Note isn't something we grow out of as we become better readers. Rather, it can help us all analyze and appreciate the author's craft in the most daunting and complex texts. Signposts give students an accessible way to understand and analyze those texts, no matter how complex the syntax and ideas.

Developing the Habits of Close Reading

> How can I promote more close reading in my classes?

Tips & Tricks!

If students don't have access to the printed book, they can mark up the eBook as they read. They can highlight and add notes directly to the text.

Built for Close Reading

Into Literature is built around close reading. The consumable format of the Student Edition invites students to be active readers, marking up the text as they go along. With ample margins and white space around each selection, students have the space they need to jot down notes and observations as they read—to look for things that you have asked them to find or simply to capture their own ideas, impressions, or questions.

At the beginning of the year, get students into the habit of recording informal notes as they read any text. For example, you might have them put:

- **?** a question mark next to ideas in the text they don't understand
- **✳** an asterisk next to surprising or important parts
- **!** an exclamation point to indicate ideas they disagree with
- ⬭ a circle around unfamiliar words or phrases
- *LOL* an LOL! next to humorous characters, events, or ideas

Students should also get into the habit of doing more purposeful annotation, using the carefully crafted guided reading questions in the Student Edition. These questions prompt students to dig back into the text to look for specific skills-focused elements, fully aligned to the skills covered in the lesson.

---

manner that fully revealed her <u>apprehension</u> 💬 . She was an apt woman; and a little experience soon demonstrated, to her satisfaction, that education and slavery were incompatible with each other.

From this time I was most narrowly watched. If I was in a separate room any [...] th of time, I was sure to [...] aving a book, and was at [...] e an account of myself, [...] was too late. The first [...] en. Mistress, in teaching [...] had given me the inch, [...] could prevent me from taking the *ell.*

These sentences help to show the considerable scrutiny that the author was under at all times. He had to be careful of being discovered.

View in Panel   Save and Close

ANALYZE AUTOBIOGRAPHY

Annotate: Highlight details in paragraph 2 that describe Douglass's mistress.

Infer: Highlight this question text and add your responses as a note.

What might Douglass's purpose be in devoting so much space to describing his mistress?

Text in Focus Video
Learn about analyzing the language in the narrative.

I was now about twelve years old, and the thought of being *a slave for life* began to bear heavily upon my heart. Just about this time, I got hold of a book entitled "The Columbian Orator."[4] Every opportunity I got, I used to read this book. Among much of other interesting matter, I found in it a dialogue between a master and his slave. The slave was represented as having run away from his master three times. The dialogue represented the conversation which took place between them, when the slave was retaken the third time. In this dialogue, the whole argument in behalf of slavery was brought forward by the master, all of which was disposed of by the slave. The slave was made to say some very sma[...] things wh[...] conversat[...] on the pa[...]

[4] "The Colu[...]

ANALYZE STRUCTURE

Annotate: In paragraphs 5 and 6, mark details about the texts Douglass read at age 12 that were especially important to him.

Cause/Effect: What effect did reading these texts have on Douglass?

Analyze Structure

In an autobiography, authors often choose to focus on events that are related by **cause and effect,** which means that one event brings about another event or creates a change in attitude. Paragraphs may be structured to show these cause-and-effect relationships, even in narratives told in chronological order.

As you read, note how the cause-and-effect structure helps Douglass achieve his purpose. Use a chart like the one below.

CAUSE	EFFECT

Modeling Close Reading

> How can I make sure that my students know what effective, purposeful annotation looks like?

Show Annotation in Action

Into Literature doesn't just ask or invite students to annotate the text. The program also provides clear models of effective, purposeful annotation. Reviewing these models as a whole class can help students better understand what close reading looks and sounds like. Try these suggestions:

● At the start of every lesson, students will see an annotation model, **Annotation in Action**. It highlights one of the skills in the lesson and models effective text markup and annotation. Discuss this model before students read the text. As a next step, you might model the process as you read the first one or two paragraphs of the text aloud. Then invite volunteers to try it out on the next paragraphs.

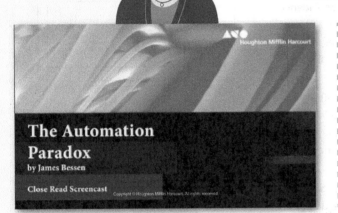

The Automation Paradox
by James Bessen

Close Read Screencast

Copyright © Houghton Mifflin Harcourt. All rights reserved.

Annotation in Action

Here are one reader's notes on the author's claim. As you read, note how the author presents his claim, reasons, and evidence.

> But these fears are misplaced—what's happening with automation is not so simple or obvious. It turns out that workers will have greater employment opportunities if their occupation undergoes some degree of computer automation. As long as they can learn to use the new tools, automation will be their friend.

The author seems to be taking a position here. Could this be his claim?

Close Read Practice Page

The Automation Paradox
by James Bessen

Do a close read of paragraph 11 by marking the text and answering the following questions.

The Automation Paradox	Close Read Notes
Paragraph 11	1. Reread paragraph 11. Make a list of words or phrases that are unclear to you. Work with a partner and outside resources to become familiar with the language or concepts.
	2. The second sentence includes the idea that *the burdens of automation fall most heavily on those least able and least equipped to deal with it.* What does the author mean by *burdens of automation*? Refer to the paragraph for context.
	3. The fourth sentence explains that some community colleges work with employers to teach skills in the classroom that students will also use in their jobs. Do you think this is a good idea? Explore reasons why or why not.

● **Ed** Certain texts in each unit feature **Close Read Screencasts**—modeled discussions about a key part of the text. You might view the screencast as a class and point out the kinds of details that the readers observe and discuss.

● **Ed** Students can hone their close-reading skills through frequent practice. Each text with a Close Read Screencast also includes a printable **Close Read Practice** activity, which is available on the platform. Have students complete the activity independently or in small groups.

● Extend the practice by having pairs of students record their own close read video about another part of text (their choice!) using screencast software.

How does *Into Literature* support close analysis and text-based responses?

Use the Text-Dependent Questions and Prompts

Close reading is just the start of reading and responding critically. In addition to getting your students to read the text closely and understand what an author is saying, you want them to analyze the texts and support their analysis and inferences with evidence from that text.

Into Literature provides a wealth of opportunities for students to demonstrate their close and careful reading. Here are some features you can use to build students' proficiency with text-dependent analysis.

- The **Analyze the Text** questions after each selection call on students to reach back into the text for evidence that supports their analysis. Whether you have students answer these questions in writing or as part of class discussion, challenge them to cite specific details to support their responses.

- Assign one or more of the **Choices** activities after reading. These activities focus on writing, media, speaking and listening, and research—and they require students to incorporate details from the text into their work.

- 😊*Ed* Use the **Response Log**, located at the back of the Student Edition, to help students capture details from each text that relate to the Essential Question for the unit. Or students might use the interactive version on Ed. This practice sets students up for success on the end-of-unit writing task, which requires them to synthesize information and cite evidence from multiple texts.

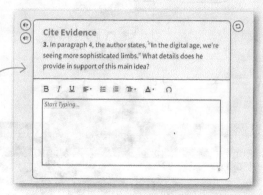

Cite Evidence

3. In paragraph 4, the author states, "In the digital age, we're seeing more sophisticated limbs." What details does he provide in support of this main idea?

Start Typing...

Unit 3 Response Log

Use this Response Log to record your ideas about how each of the texts in Unit 3 relates to or comments on the **Essential Question**.

ESSENTIAL QUESTION
? How do you find courage in the face of fear?

Selection title	Type your notes in the boxes provided.
from The Breadwinner	
Life Doesn't Frighten Me	
Fears and Phobias	
Wired for Fear	
Embarrassed? Blame Your Brain	

😊*Ed*
Tips & Tricks!

If students use the digital annotation tools to mark evidence as they read, those annotations collect in the Notes panel of their eBook. Students can then review their annotations and Response Logs as they draft their writing for end-of-unit tasks. See **Building Better Writers** on page 78 to learn more about how the digital writing experience in **Writable** supports students in weaving evidence into their work.

Writable

Writing
Disaster-Film Proposal

How would you turn this suspenseful story into a disaster movie? Write a three- to four-paragraph proposal for a film based on "Rogue Wave." Include each of the following:

- a clear controlling idea or thesis statement
- details of the opening scene, establishing the characters, setting, and conflict
- a description of each important scene in the plot

Speaking & Listening
Critique the Poem

Review "Icarus's Flight" and think about its conversational tone. Then work with a partner to analyze its content.

- Take turns reading the poem aloud. As your partner reads, take notes on the questions asked throughout the poem. What is the purpose of these questions? Can you relate to Icarus's struggle and goals?

- With your partner, review your notes and prepare your analysis. Be sure to include examples to support your ideas and to make your points clear.

- Share your views with the class in an oral critique.

Close Reading and Notice & Note

> I'm interested in using Notice & Note as a close reading strategy. How does *Into Literature* support Notice & Note?

Complementary Approaches

Maybe you're already using Notice & Note as a close reading strategy. Or maybe it's something you've heard about and are interested to learn how to incorporate it into your close reading, without pulling you away from all the things you need to do, week to week. If so, *Into Literature* is the perfect program for you. Notice & Note is built right into our program.

Working closely with Notice & Note creators Kylene Beers and Robert Probst, *Into Literature* provides you with all the tools that you need to implement this accessible and powerful close reading protocol.

Use the resources in your Student and Teacher's Edition to get started with Notice & Note. Go online to find additional resources, from **Peer Coach Videos** and **Anchor Charts** to **Writing Frames for Fiction and Nonfiction**, to support and reinforce your instruction.

Tips & Tricks!

To learn more about using Notice & Note for close reading, see pages 66–71.

meltdowns and abrupt time-outs. Former blogger Tavi Gevinson has confessed: "I wanted to reap fame's benefits without feeling like my life would become a video game of winning people over and seeking attention." Another former influencer stated in her parting message: "I found myself drowning in the illusion. . . . Social media isn't real. It's purely contrived images and edited clips ranked against each other. It's a system based on social approval, likes and dislikes, validation in views, success in followers . . . it's perfectly orchestrated judgment. And it consumed me." Being a social media influencer is often harder than it looks, and often not all it

NOTICE & NOTE
QUOTED WORDS

When you notice the author has quoted the conclusions of someone who was a participant in an event, you've found a **Quoted Words** signpost.

Notice & Note: Mark the quotations in paragraph 7.

Analyze: Why was this person quoted or cited and what did this add?

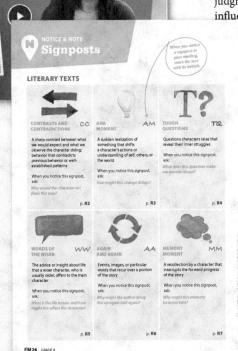

Aha Moment
A sudden realization of something that shifts a character's actions or understanding of self, others, or the world

Memory Moment
A recollection by a character that interrupts the forward progress of the story.

Text Clues
• A character has a flashback that interrupts the present.
• "I suddenly remembered. . ." or "Thinking back. . ."
• A character tells an old story from the past.

Ask Yourself
Why might this memory be important?

The answer to this question can tell you more about a **character** or a possible **theme**, or it can foreshadow what's to come later in the **plot**.

Outcomes & Growth

Building Better Writers

Writable

I'm not experienced at teaching writing. Help!

Into Literature Has You Covered

If you lack confidence in your ability to teach writing, you're not alone. It's a challenge for most of us to put well-crafted sentences and paragraphs on paper, let alone teach others how to do it well. Yet, with the right resources and tools, you can succeed. (Yes, *really*.)

Those writing resources and tools are built into every aspect of *Into Literature*. Here are some ideas for using the resources in the program to build writing into your daily classroom routines.

- **Kick off with quickwrites.** Begin each unit by having students quickwrite in response to the illustration and the Essential Question. Students can jot down their ideas within the **Spark Your Learning** pages in the Student Edition. Quickwriting is also an effective way to launch each lesson. Find inspiration and prompts within the **Engage Your Brain** feature at the start of each lesson.

- **Offer opportunities to write about the reading.** The **Respond** section after each lesson in the Student Edition includes a variety of writing activities. Students can write in response to the **Analyze the Text** questions or the **Choices** prompts that follow.

- **Build toward a cumulative task.** The writing task at the end of each unit prompts students to synthesize what they've learned across the texts and share new insights in different modes, including arguments, expository texts, and narratives. Students can prepare for this end-of-unit task by recording notes about the Essential Question in their **Response Logs**, located in the back of the Student Edition.

- ⚙️ **Ed** **Use Writable.** All of the writing assignments within the Student Edition—plus a library of additional connected prompts—are available in **Writable**, which you can access from Ed: Your Friend in Learning. Writable's peer review function drives the revision process, which helps students grow as writers. And time-saving tools like Revision Aid and Turn It In support teachers.

Connecting Reading & Writing

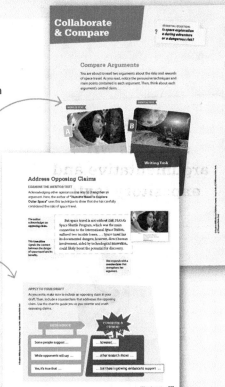

Share Models and Examples

One effective way to connect reading and writing is to expose students to strong models of each form. The instructional design of *Into Literature* helps you make that connection.

- Each unit includes one or more **mentor texts**—authentic examples of the form that students are responsible for writing as part of the cumulative task. As students read and analyze the mentor texts, they are prompted to look at aspects of the writer's craft.

- The end-of-unit task reinforces this reading-writing connection by having students revisit specific techniques used by the writers of the mentor texts. Challenge students to use these techniques in their own writing.

- 😊**Ed** The **Interactive Writing Lessons** on our platform include examples—both strong and weak—of student writing. Consider projecting these models and using them in a whole-class discussion and peer review.

> **What tips do you have for closely connecting reading and writing?**

Review the Prompt and Rubric

Take the time to familiarize students with the destination before they embark on each end-of-unit writing journey. Here's how:

- As a class, review the writing prompt at the beginning of the task. Ask: What is the purpose and format of the writing? Who is the audience? Encourage students to underline or circle key details in the prompt that clarify the assignment.

- Examine each bulleted characteristic in the rubric on second page of the task. Explain any unfamiliar terms to students, and invite them to offer examples.

- Review the mentor text, depending on how recently you taught it. Consider asking students to explain how the mentor text exemplifies different characteristics listed in the rubric.

> **How can I make sure my students know what's expected of their writing?**

😊**Ed**

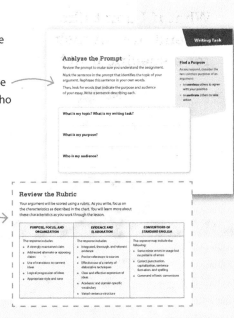

Tips & Tricks!

Ⓦritable

Assign the **Analyze the Mentor Text** prompt in each unit to inspire deeper analysis of writer's craft.

Focusing on Key Writing Modes

How can I help students write argumentative and expository texts?

Provide Frequent Practice

Writing effective arguments and expository texts is critically important—for success on high-stakes assessments, in college, and in the workplace. You can help students achieve success by giving them frequent practice in these modes.

- If you preview all the prompts and tasks within *Into Literature*, you'll notice more opportunities to write arguments and expository texts than other forms. Look for occasions to change the focus or complexity of instruction at different points in the year. For instance, if students are writing an argument in September, they might focus on the basics—claim, support, and counterclaims. An assignment later in the year might challenge students to use rhetorical devices for persuasive effect.

- Use the scaffolding and graphic organizers in the Student Edition to support students in honing their skills in these modes.

- ☺**Ed** Prepare students for the cumulative task by assigning only prompts in that form over the course of the unit. Within **Writable**, you will find an additional prompt for each text that "ladders up" to the end-of-unit task.

Exploring Your Options

What if I don't like the end-of-unit task for a specific unit?

Consider the Alternatives

Don't feel limited by the writing task or mode featured in each unit. *Into Literature* has alternatives for those who want to chart a different course.

- Consult the end-of-unit task **Planning Guides** in your Teacher's Edition for a list of other cumulative assignments you might consider.

- Check the **Reflect & Extend** feature in the Student Edition for a writing prompt focused on a different mode. If you are looking for more instruction to support the assignment, use the **Interactive Writing Lessons** on the platform.

- The **Reflect & Extend** feature also includes a unit **Media Project**—a great opportunity to experiment with project-based learning in your classroom. Find step-by-step support for each project online. Even if you lack the technology or the time to devote to an extended project, you might assign a low-tech or no-tech option. Storyboarding, scripting, and sketchnoting are all valuable writing opportunities for students.

- ☺**Ed** Can't find what you are looking for? Create your own prompt or assignment in **Writable**.

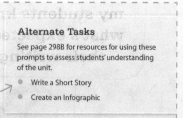

Alternate Tasks

See page 298B for resources for using these prompts to assess students' understanding of the unit.

- Write a Short Story
- Create an Infographic

Supporting Students with Key Skills

How do I help my students with tricky skills like citing text evidence and synthesizing across texts?

Reinforce the Fundamentals

Even seasoned writers can struggle with skills like citing text evidence and synthesizing across texts. Carve out class time to provide targeted teaching and practice in these fundamental skills. Here are some resources in the program that can help you:

Citing Text Evidence

- As a class, review the **Peer Coach Video** on citing text evidence. Then have students practice the **ACE** method—**A**nswer, **C**ite, **E**xplain. Encourage them to use this method when jotting down brief responses to questions about the texts they are reading, as well as in more formal writing assignments.

- Display the **Anchor Chart** that accompanies the Peer Coach video as a visual reminder of this method. Find a printable version of the chart on Ed. Consider also displaying some sentence starters that students can use to weave text evidence into their writing. As a class, brainstorm additional sentence starters to add to the sticky notes shown.

In the first paragraph, the text states that . . .

The writer emphasizes that . . .

According to the text, . . .

These lines prove that . . .

By stating . . . . the writer asserts . . .

- For independent practice, assign **Interactive Writing Lessons: Using Textual Evidence**.

Synthesizing Across Texts

- To review the skill, show the **Peer Coach Video** on synthesis, as well as printing and distributing the corresponding **Anchor Chart**.

- At the beginning of each unit, review the **Response Log** in the back of the Student Edition. Then, after students read each text, have them revisit the Essential Question, using the chart to note how that text relates to the question. Prompt them to record their opinions and insights, as well as direct quotations from the text. This practice will set students up for success in synthesizing information across the texts as part of the cumulative writing task.

- Use the **Collaborate & Compare** lessons in each unit to help students practice synthesizing information across two texts. The project at the end of the **Collaborate & Compare** gives students the perfect opportunity.

Tips & Tricks!

Have students record notes in the interactive **Response Log** in their eBooks. They can also use the annotation tools to capture additional notes as they read each text. **Writable** allows students to view those notes alongside their draft to support them in synthesizing information and citing text evidence.

> **What are the best ways for students to get feedback on their work?**

Build in Time for Self, Peer, and Teacher Review

Rarely (or ever!) does a first draft reflect the well-reasoned argument or suspenseful narrative we envisioned so clearly in our minds. Writing is a process: Our words, sentences, and ideas gain power and precision through extensive revision. That revision can be inspired by our own "fresh read" of our draft and by helpful suggestions from peers.

Here are some steps you can take to establish a culture of feedback in your classroom.

Self Review

- Build in class time for students to review their own drafts. The **Revision Guide** for each end-of-unit writing task in the Student Edition breaks down this process. Use the **Peer Review in Action** feature to model how to use the Revision Guide.

- **Ed** If students are using **Writable** to complete their drafts, remind them to consult the writer's checklist before they submit their work.

- For major writing assignments, use one or two class periods for a "revise-a-palooza" activity. Set up stations around the classroom, with each station focused on a different aspect of writing—introduction, body paragraphs, conclusion, elaboration, transitions, and so on. Have small groups of students spend 10 minutes at each station, revising their drafts with that focus.

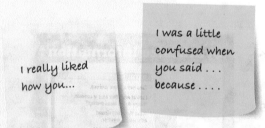

Peer Review

- As a class, generate a list of sentence starters that students can use when they review their peers' drafts. Display these sentence starters on the wall. Ask students to use several of the starters each time they undertake a peer review.

- I really liked how you...

- I was a little confused when you said . . . because . . . .

- One way to grab your readers' attention would be to . . .

- Another piece of evidence you can include is . . .

- Your writing would be easier to understand if you added transitions like . . .

- Your organization would be clearer if you . . .

- **Ed** Use the anonymous peer-review function in **Writable** to add an element of fun to the process of revision. Set up the assignment so that each student reviews the drafts of multiple peers. Encourage reviewers to use the comment stems to provide concrete feedback. Then challenge students to use their classmates' suggestions to revise their work.

Conferences

- Make the time to confer with your students about their drafts. Use the **Quick Check** prompts in your Teacher's Edition to support your students at each stage of the end-of-unit writing task.

- You might circulate around the room as you check in on individuals. Another option is to meet with each student as the rest of the class participates in peer review or "revise-a-palooza."

Saving Time

> How can I spend less time grading student writing?

Set Yourself Up for Success

Ever feel buried under the weight of student essays waiting for your review? If you let yourself, you can spend your weekends and evenings trying to keep up with the onerous job of grading student writing. Don't do it! Instead, use these practical tips, tools, and tricks to make grading more manageable.

- **Don't grade every assignment.** Reserve grading for major assignments, such as end-of-unit writing tasks and practice for summative assessments. For lower-stakes assignments, such as **Choices** prompts after each lesson, peer and self review can suffice.

- **Rely on peer review.** Remember—peer review can also help *you*. The comments, feedback, and ratings of peers can serve as a gauge for you to consider in your grading of major assignments.

- **Leverage time-saving digital tools.** The tools embedded within **Writable** are designed to make grading a little bit easier for you. Activate **Turn It In** to check the originality of students' work. Consult AI-powered **Revision Aid** to get paragraph-level feedback on the ideas, organization, and language in each draft. Use the comment stems provided to help you compose your feedback. You can also create your own comment stems for future use.

- **Use data and reports.** Let the data drive the focus of your review. Use the reports in **Writable** to track students' proficiency with skills connected to standards. Then use this targeted lens to grade students' writing assignments.

Integrating Speaking & Listening

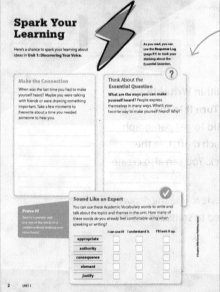

How can I make sure that my students have productive discussions about literature?

Engage Their Brains

As a comprehensive literature program, *Into Literature* contains ample instructional support and abundant opportunities for speaking and listening. We know that in a typical week, a sizable part of your classroom time is spent having discussions. By using *Into Literature's* features, you can ensure that students have productive discussions that are not only helping them master ELA concepts but also building their competency in communicating ideas clearly and responding to ideas that might be very different from their own.

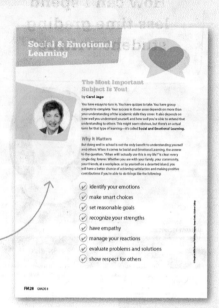

- At the beginning of the year, do a whole-class reading of the essay **"The Most Important Subject Is You"** by Carol Jago, which appears in the Student Edition on pages FM28–FM31. Review and discuss the strategies for effective conversations and discussions. Generate ground rules for your classroom community, which you may want to display on the wall.

- Use the **Spark Your Learning** and **Engage Your Brain** activities at the beginning of each unit and lesson to hook and engage students. These brief, informal opportunities for discussion can help to ease students into the lesson or make personal connections to ideas in the text.

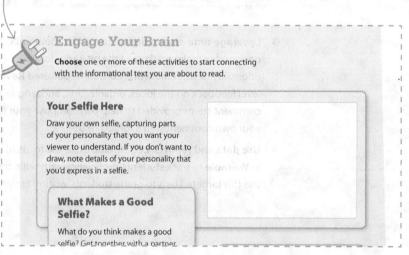

- After students finish reading each text, have them discuss the **Turn and Talk** prompt with a classmate. Encourage sharing of ideas and perspectives in a whole-class discussion before moving on to more sophisticated textual analysis.

Talking About the Text

How can I use speaking and listening to support more in-depth analysis of a text?

Make Time for More Structured Activities

Informal classroom discussions can be a great way to get the ball rolling, but students can also use more formal, structured opportunities to practice higher-level skills. After every selection, in the **Choices** section, you will always have an option to assign a speaking and listening activity as an end-of-selection assessment. These activities are more stepped-out and structured, containing suggestions for purposeful speaking and effective and constructive listening.

Notice that many of these activities also support social and emotional learning. Speaking and listening activities are great opportunities for students to work on SEL competencies.

Speaking & Listening
↳ Present a Sonnet

Prepare a sonnet for an oral reading. Find a sonnet online that you would like to present. When you and your classmates read your sonnets aloud, provide thoughtful feedback to each other.

. Experiment
ples to bring
e text.

l with your
ressions and
he meaning

ud to

Social & Emotional Learning
↳ Discuss with a Small Group

What could Mister Toussaint teach his neighbors about dealing with a prank like LOONY GOONY? Work with a group to create a set of helpful tips.

- As a group, review the story and note Mister Toussaint's actions in response to LOONY GOONY. Discuss which actions were effective and which were ineffective or destructive, and why.

- Brainstorm a list of tips or guidelines that would help someone overcome a similar "Internet of Things prank."

- Together, organize everyone's ideas into a set of step-by-step instructions for what a person should do if faced with something like LOONY GOONY.

Interflora 35

🙂 **Ed**

Share Models and Examples

Speaking and listening are skills that you have to see in action to fully understand. That makes *Into Literature's* speaking and listening interactive lessons a vital part of our coverage. Encourage students to go online to see instruction and models of effective collaboration, discussion, and presenting. Or, you might share these models in a whole-class lesson. Have students identify characteristics of strong discussions and presentations.

What Does a Collaborative Discussion Sound Like?

Listen in on this small group discussion, a meeting of the members of a class discussion group. See if you can spot students' constructive—and disruptive—discussion behaviors.

1. Show Up Ready   01:28

What Makes a Dynamic Presentation?

This speaker was assigned to give an informal demonstration of the verbal and nonverbal elements of speech delivery. View each segment of her presentation and respond to the questions.

How can I promote more collaboration in my classroom?

Collaboration: A Skill for the Future

Whether you're teaching middle school or high school, you know that you have to prepare students for a future in which collaboration is going to be a key to success. The ability to work effectively in teams is growing in importance, both in college and on the job. Your ELA classroom is where students will receive some of the best and more relevant practice with this skill.

An entire strand of *Into Literature*—**Collaborate & Compare**—supports collaborative group work. Students are still asked to read and analyze each text on their own or with the entire class. But as a final wrap-up assignment, they will work together as a team on a collaborative project. All of these projects require that students hone their speaking and listening skills.

Keep the following tips in mind when using these collaborative activities in your classroom.

- **Make the time.** These lessons take precious instructional time, but they are worth it. Students have the opportunity to flex various muscles, from collaboration and synthesis to research and presentation.

- **Keep peer groups small.** Each group should contain between four and six students. Smaller sizes allow for more focused collaboration, with each student playing a critical role in the work.

- **Let groups showcase their work.** Build in time for presentation, sharing, and reflection at the end of the assignment. Groups should feel proud of their work!

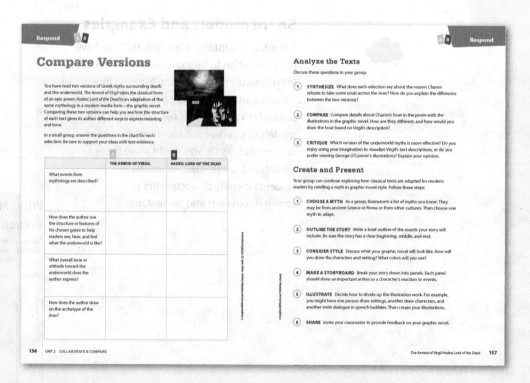

Using Speaking and Listening in Summative Tasks

How can I get students to engage in more extended speaking and listening activities?

Tips & Tricks!

Each end-of-unit speaking and listening task includes point-of-use links to more support and instruction. Students can use these digital resources to find extra help, or you might use the resources to deliver a whole-class minilesson on relevant speaking and listening skills.

It Doesn't Have to Be a Writing Assignment

A lot of students don't like to write papers—probably most of them, in fact. But you know that some students in your class love to get up and talk in front of the class or engage in a spirited debate. And some students need more practice in these areas. With *Into Literature*, the end-of-unit assignment doesn't have to be another paper. It can be something that allows some of your more outspoken students to shine, and that gives some of your quieter students a clear and structured assignment to nudge them out of their comfort zone and to help them on their way to becoming poised and confident presenters.

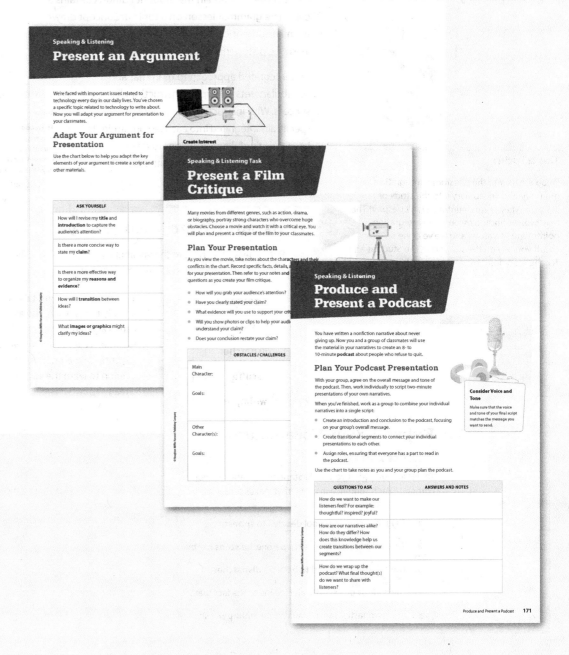

Integrating Grammar and Vocabulary into Your Lessons

Getting Started

> **How does *Into Literature* help me teach grammar and vocabulary in context?**

Tips & Tricks!

If you are new to the classroom, integrating grammar and vocabulary into the study of literature may seem daunting. Don't despair! The hard work is finding meaningful integration points with literature, and we've done that for you. If you rely on the support in the Student and Teacher's Edition, you've got everything you need.

An Integrated Approach

Grammar and vocabulary are integrated directly into our program. Coverage begins with the Student Edition. Every prose selection in the Student Edition contains a complete grammar lesson on a topic or concept drawn from an authentic text. Also, carefully chosen "words to learn" help students expand their vocabulary as they read.

This integrated approach to grammar and vocabulary sets you up for instructional success. With instruction and practice specifically integrated into each lesson, students have meaningful opportunities to relate grammar and word choice to author's craft.

Watch Your Language!

Types of Clauses

An **adjective clause,** or **relative clause,** is a subordinate clause that is used as an adjective. It usually follows the noun or pronoun it modifies in a sentence. An adjective clause is often introduced by a relative pronoun such as *that, which, who, whom,* or *whose.* An adjective clause can also be introduced by a subordinating conjunction such as *until, after, where, when, because,* or *although.*

Watch Your Language!

Imperative Mood

The **mood** of a verb refers to the manner in which the action or state of being is expressed. A verb is in the **imperative mood** when it is part of a command or request. In an imperative sentence, the subject is always implied or understood to be *you.* These sentences from "My Favorite Chaperone" are in the imperative mood.

"Take off your jacket and hang it up, Nurzhan."

"Let me try to get permission for you from Papa."

Expand Your Vocabulary

Put a check mark next to the vocabulary words that you feel comfortable using when speaking or writing.

sponsor	☐
stun	☐
dispatcher	☐
scuffle	☐
whimper	☐

Turn to a partner and talk about the words you already know. Then, use as many words as you can in a paragraph about the way your parents or guardians expect you to behave. As you read "My Favorite Chaperone," use the definitions in the side column to learn the vocabulary words you don't already know.

Expand Your Vocabulary

PRACTICE AND APPLY

To demonstrate that you understand the vocabulary words, complete each sentence in a way that makes sense.

1. The civics club at school decided to **sponsor** . . .

2. When Nurzhan is Maya's chaperone, he **stuns** her by . . .

3. The cab driver needed to have his **dispatcher** . . .

4. The sounds of a **scuffle** alerted me to the fact that . . .

5. At a gymnastics meet, Maya might **whimper** if she . . .

Diving More Deeply Into Grammar

What if I want to dig deeper into a grammatical topic?

⊙ Ed
Interactive Grammar
Lesson: Kinds of Clauses

A Systematic Approach

Sometimes, it helps to reinforce grammatical concepts outside the context of literature. After all, that's where students can get deeper instruction and practice. *Into Literature* contains a full online grammar, usage, and mechanics program—**Interactive Grammar Lessons**—covering the full range of topics. Each lesson contains clear, direct instruction (with models and examples) and a full range of engaging practice opportunities that provide immediate and clear feedback to students.

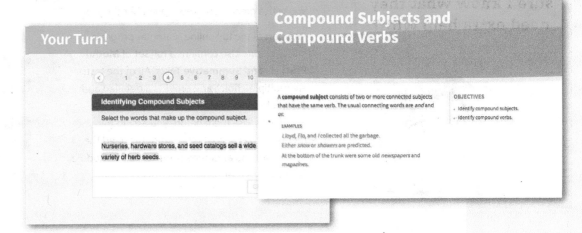

Throughout the Student Edition, there are point-of-use references to these online tutorials, which allow students to get valuable reteaching opportunities or extra practice.

Into Literature also offers the **Grammar Practice Workbook**. This student consumable contains all of the topics covered in the online grammar program, but in a friendly format, so that students can practice wherever and whenever they want. Each lesson begins with a quick refresher on the topic, followed by grade-appropriate practice. The lessons are also available as editable Word files, so that you can customize and adapt them as you see fit.

ΔƎ◇ HMH (Into) Literature™

Grammar Practice

Grade 7

MODULE 6: THE CLAUSE
INDEPENDENT AND SUBORDINATE CLAUSES

6a A *clause* is a group of words that contains a verb and its subject.

Every clause contains a subject and a verb. However, not all clauses express complete thoughts.

SENTENCE   David Wagoner is a poet and a teacher who lives in Ohio. [complete thought]
                S   V

CLAUSE   **David Wagoner is** a poet and a teacher. [complete thought]
                S   V

CLAUSE   **who lives** in Ohio [incomplete thought]

There are two kinds of clauses, *independent* and *subordinate*.

6b An *independent* (or *main*) *clause* expresses a complete thought and can stand by itself as a sentence.
                S   V

**EXERCISE 1   Identifying Independent Clauses and
                Subordinate Clauses**

On the line before each sentence, write *indep.* if the italicized clause is an independent clause or *sub.* if it is a subordinate clause.

EX.   _sub._   1. Ramona told me a joke *that I really enjoyed.*

_____   1. Albert brought the sandwiches, and *May Ellen made the punch.*

_____   2. *Since you've been away,* the neighborhood has really changed.

_____   3. I don't remember *where I put my jacket.*

_____   4. *Virgil planted the flowers* that are blooming in my garden.

_____   5. The student *who sits behind me in science class* moved here from Mexico last month.

_____   6. Monday or Tuesday, *whichever day you choose,* is fine.

_____   7. *The bride and bridegroom wore the Hmong wedding costume* that they brought from Laos.

_____   8. *After they left their native country,* they decided to live in Rome.

> How can I assess my students to make sure I know what they need extra help with?

Use the Diagnostic and Summative Assessments

At the beginning of the year, you can use the **Diagnostic Screening Tests**, available on the platform, to get a high-level assessment of student strengths and knowledge gaps in grammatical concepts. It's a multiple-choice test in two parts, each with 50 questions. This will provide you with a great "starting-out point" for the year.

As a part of the full online grammar program, *Into Literature* also contains a full set of **Module Pretests and Summative Test**s. All of the tests are multiple-choice and provide a detailed and comprehensive assessment before and after instruction. Use them before you assign the modules (to assess whether students need the extra help) and after they complete each module (to ensure mastery).

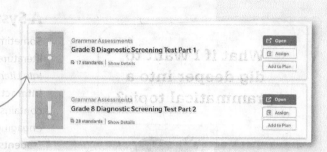

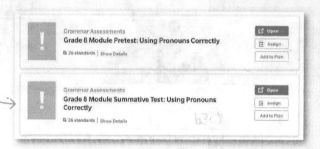

> How can I make sure that my students are ready for the writing assessment at the end of the year?

Yes, Students Will Be Scored on Their Language

We know that grammar is a critical part of the ELA curriculum, all year round. But we also know that many students will be held accountable for their mastery of this topic at a critical point of the year: in an end-of-year writing assessment. To help them prepare for this, each end-of-unit task contains an integrated editing lesson focused on a specific grammatical topic. Use these targeted lessons to build students' proficiency in key language skills.

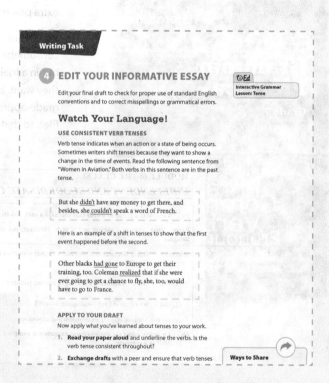

Targeting the Areas of Need

What words should my students focus on learning?

Focus on High-Utility Words

In each prose selection, a manageable list of high-utility words have been selected as target vocabulary. Introduce the words before reading, using the **Expand Your Vocabulary** feature to help students assess their own knowledge of the words.

When they see each word in context, students are given a clear, content-appropriate definition and guidance on pronunciation. Following the reading, you can use the vocabulary activity in the **Respond** section to help students practice using the words in writing and discussion.

Expand Your Vocabulary

Put a check mark next to the vocabulary words that you feel comfortable using when speaking or writing.

- saturated ☐
- indulgent ☐
- narcissist ☐
- intimacy ☐
- eternity ☐

Turn to a partner and talk about the vocabulary words you already know. Then, answer this question: *Are selfies good for you?* Use as many vocabulary words as you can in your answer. As you read the following arguments, use the definitions in the side column to learn the vocabulary words you don't already know.

---

2 In a society **saturated,** stuffed to the brim, with social media, selfies are an artistic form of self-expression. Humans, since the beginning of time, have used self-portraits to express themselves. From ancient Egypt to the early Greeks to famous painters such as Rembrandt and van Gogh,[1] people have expressed themselves artistically through self-portraits.

3 The only difference between the artists of old and modern selfie-takers is that technology now allows anyone and everyone to be an artist, and a "self-portrait" is now called a "selfie." It's easy to create a "self-portrait" with a smart phone and its filters. You don't

saturated
(săch´ə-rāt´əd) *adj.* Something that is *saturated* is filled until it is unable to hold or contain more.

How can I teach strategies that support students' own independent vocabulary acquisition?

Provide Instruction on Strategies

Direct instruction for high-frequency words is useful, but students will acquire most of their vocabulary independently. What can you do to ensure that students have the right tools to build their own knowledge? All of our vocabulary instruction in the Student Edition is paired with a vocabulary acquisition strategy that students can deploy as needed. Devote time to these instructional opportunities and assign the **Practice & Apply** activities to reinforce each strategy you've taught.

Vocabulary Strategy
Context Clues

Interactive Vocabulary Lesson: Context Clues

One way to figure out an unfamiliar word's meaning is to use **context clues,** or hints found in the surrounding text. Here is an example:

> There are critics who say that selfies are taken only by narcissists craving attention.

To figure out the meaning of *narcissists,* note the words *craving attention* that appear after the unfamiliar word. These words hint that narcissists are people who crave attention.

PRACTICE AND APPLY

Find an unfamiliar word in each of the texts. Use clues to help you determine each word's meaning.

But what about when students are reading with more independence?

Have Students Track Their Vocabulary

Ideally, students are reading out of class, independently, in subject areas that interest them the most. And that is one of the best times for students to work on mastering unfamiliar words. The **HMH Study Guides** all include Vocabulary Tracker word logs that students can customize to their needs.

If students are reading a novel or longer work of your choice, challenge them to find a certain number of unfamiliar words as they read and log their findings in a chart. For each word, students can include a definition, a sentence using the word, and a picture that exemplifies the word and its meaning.

STUDY GUIDE

The Crossover by Kwame Alexander

VOCABULARY TRACKER

Use the chart below to record unfamiliar terms that you encounter while reading. Choose words that you are likely to use in future reading, writing, and class discussions in this and other classes. Page references will vary depending on the edition of the book you are reading.

Word	Page	Definition from Context	Dictionary Definition	My New Sentence
acclaimed	4	Something acclaimed is probably good.	Praised in public	LeBron James's skill was acclaimed around the world.

How can I support students' vocabulary needs regardless of the text I'm teaching in class?

Use the Interactive Lessons

We know that you have your own texts that you want to teach, based on current events or your sense of what your unique students are interested in. The **Interactive Vocabulary Lessons** are there to support you and your students. The lessons cover the full range of vocabulary strategies, including ample coverage of word roots and affixes.

Analyzing Word Structure

Many words can be broken into smaller parts. These word parts include base words, roots, prefixes, and suffixes.

Read these points to learn more about word structure.

Base Words

A **base word** is a word part that by itself is also a word. Other words or word parts can be added to base words to form new words.

Specific Context Clues

Type of Clue	Key Words/Phrases	Example
Definition or restatement of the meaning of the word	or, which is, that is, in other words, also known as, also called	Most chemicals are *toxic*, or poisonous.
Example following an unfamiliar word	such as, like, as if, for example, especially, including	*Amphibians*, such as frogs and salamanders, live in the pond by our house.
Comparison with a more familiar word or concept	as, like, also, similar to, in the same way, likewise	Like the rest of my *frugal* family, I always save most of the money I earn.

Prefixes

A **prefix** is a word part attached to the beginning of a word. Most prefixes come from Greek, Latin, or Old English.

Prefix	Meaning	Example
mal-	bad or wrong	**mal**function
micro-	small or short	**micro**scope
semi-	half	**semi**circle

Incorporating Academic Vocabulary

How can I improve my students' knowledge of academic vocabulary?

Teach Words That Will Make a Difference

Academic vocabulary words (sometimes referred to as Tier 2 words) show up across academic disciplines—math, science, social studies, ELA—in lessons and assessments. For example, at any point in the day students might be asked to "analyze" a poem or a political speech or a graph, but if they're struggling with the meaning of the word *analyze* all of those tasks are going to be more difficult. Some students will come into your class knowing these words and some will pick them up eventually through reading. But research shows that directly teaching these words and reinforcing them with practice provides real gains for students. Every unit of *Into Literature* focuses on a manageable list of topic-appropriate words that students can learn—words that will enrich their writing and speaking.

● Use the **Sound Like an Expert** activity within the **Spark Your Learning** feature to introduce the academic vocabulary words for each unit.

Prove It!
Turn to a partner and use one of the words in a sentence about technology and its successes and failures.

Sound Like an Expert

You can use these Academic Vocabulary words to write and talk about topics and themes in the unit. Which of these words do you already feel comfortable using when speaking or writing?

	I can use it!	I understand it.	I'll look it up.
commentary	☐	☐	☐
network	☐	☐	☐
occupation	☐	☐	☐
option	☐	☐	☐
speculate	☐	☐	☐

Writing
↳ Summarize a Story

Write a summary of "The Brave Little Toaster." Your summary should briefly retell the most important events of the story in your own words.

● Begin by describing the story's setting and introducing the main character, Mister Toussaint.

● Next, describe the conflict Mister Toussaint faces and how he responds to it. Tell the main events of the story in the order in which they happened.

● Explain how the conflict is resolved at the end of the story.

As you write and discuss, be sure to use the **Academic Vocabulary** words.

commentary
network
occupation
option
speculate

● Consult the Teacher's Edition notes to help you revisit these words throughout your teaching of the texts in the unit.

● As students complete the **Choices** activities after reading, challenge them to use the academic vocabulary words in their writing, discussions, and presentations.

Academic Vocabulary

Some examples of the academic vocabulary words in *Into Literature* include:

Grade 6	Grade 7	Grade 8
• consequence	• aspect	• deduce
• principle	• ensure	• network
• relevant	• valid	• technique

Assessing Student Progress & Mastery

Getting Started

> How can I get to know my students' skills—both strengths and areas for growth?

Get to Know Your Students

It's the beginning of the school year, and a sea of unfamiliar faces stares at you expectantly (or cynically!) at the beginning of each class period. Here are some tips for getting to know what skill strengths and challenges your students are bringing to the classroom:

● Use the **HMH Growth Measure**, a short screener administered three times a year, to understand each student's Lexile® level and proficiency with grade-level reading and language skills. This insight, along with information about personal interests, can help you anticipate, plan, and recommend.

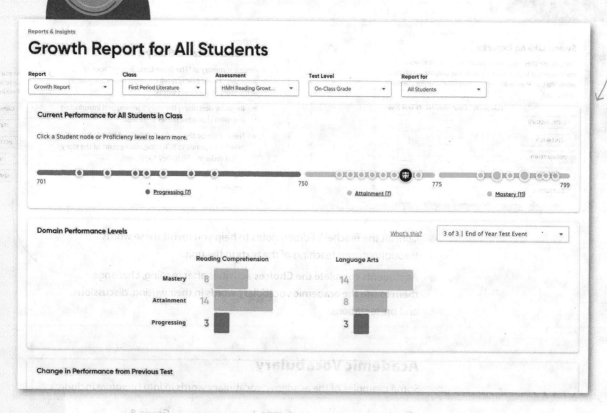

Reports & Insights

Growth Report for All Students

Report	Class	Assessment	Test Level	Report for
Growth Report	First Period Literature	HMH Reading Growt...	On-Class Grade	All Students

Current Performance for All Students in Class

Click a Student node or Proficiency level to learn more.

701 750 775 799

● Progressing (7) ● Attainment (7) ● Mastery (11)

Domain Performance Levels What's this? 3 of 3 | End of Year Test Event

	Reading Comprehension	Language Arts
Mastery	8	14
Attainment	14	8
Progressing	3	3

Change in Performance from Previous Test

● Want more data insights to round out your understanding of each student? Assign the more targeted **Diagnostic Assessments** in reading, grammar, and literature. These assessments are available on our learning platform.

● Don't forget to consult data or feedback from the last academic year. Reach out to the previous grade's teachers to find out whether there are any tips or "look for's" that you should consider as you start the year.

Setting Up Students for Success

How will my students demonstrate comprehension and mastery of skills and standards?

Monitor Progress with Formative Assessments

The embedded formative assessments in the program can help you monitor progress and check understanding. Here are some options:

- Each lesson focuses on one or two reading skills relevant to a particular genre. Use the **Get Ready** feature in the Student Edition to introduce the skills prior to reading.

- Have students apply what they learned by answering the **Guided Reading Questions** in the side margins.

- Reserve five minutes at the end of reading to have students complete the brief **Assessment Practice**. Use a show of hands or polling software to check for understanding.

- After reading, use the **Analyze the Text** questions to guide class discussions and check students' understanding of the skills.

- Use the **Quick Check** notes in the Teacher's Edition to check students' comprehension of the text. The suggestions can help you decide what to do next if students didn't understand the key ideas.

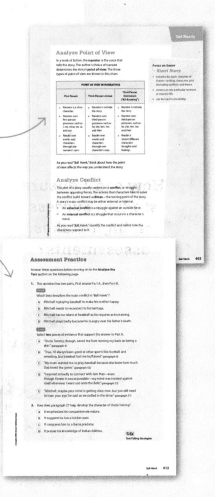

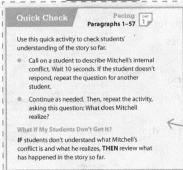

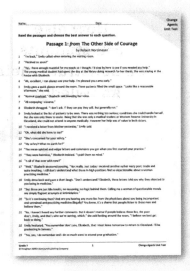

Assess Proficiency with Summative Assessments

Online you will find a library of summative assessments in both editable and interactive formats.

- Use the **Selection Tests** to assess students' mastery of the reading, vocabulary, and language skills taught in each lesson.

- Assign a **Unit Test** to gauge student proficiency with the standards covered in each unit. The **Unit Planning Guides** at the beginning of each unit in your Teacher's Edition show tested skills and standards.

- Customize any assessment to meet your instructional goals. Add, edit, or remove items from online assessments. You can also adjust the editable and printable version of the test.

Prepare for High-Stakes Assessments

Like it or not, your students' academic success depends on their performance on high-stakes assessments. The most effective preparation is embedded in daily class instruction and practice. Try these strategies:

- Use the Student Edition as built-in assessment preparation throughout the year. Questions and tasks are modeled after those items on your state assessment and on both the SAT and ACT.

- Look for technology-enhanced items and two-part questions within the Student Edition and on **Selection** and **Unit Tests**.

- Give students ample opportunities to compare and synthesize across texts. The instructional design of the Student Edition and assessments provides plenty of practice.

- Use the **audio excerpts** in Unit Tests to prepare students to sharpen their speaking and listening skills.

- Use the **Writing Task** at the end of each unit to prepare students for the writing portion of your state assessment. Prompts and rubrics provide relevant practice.

- **Ed** The end-of-unit task, along with other prompts that mirror summative writing assessments, are available to assign digitally within **Writable**.

> **How can I ensure student success on high-stakes assessments?**

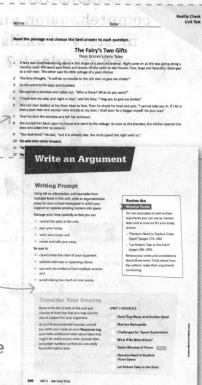

Use Performance-Based Assessments

Students can demonstrate their knowledge of what they learned in many creative ways. Here are some options:

- Assign one or more of the **Choices** activities at the end of each lesson.

- Use the **end-of-unit tasks** in the Student Edition to wrap up each unit. These tasks prompt students to synthesize ideas across texts and share their insights in writing, discussion, debate, or media, for example.

- Consult **Reflect & Extend** pages in the Student Edition for alternate options, including project-based learning opportunities.

> **How else can students demonstrate their knowledge?**

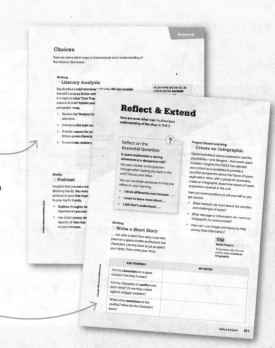

Using Data to Inform Instruction

Learn to Look for Patterns

Into Literature provides a mine of information at your fingertips, so long as you know where and what to look for. Start your investigation on the platform.

How can I use data in my planning and differentiation?

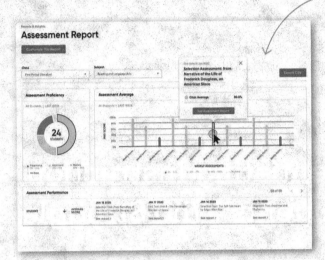

- Consult the **Assessment Report** to see students' overall mastery on all completed assessments. Look at most-missed items and standards before digging in to investigate further.

- View the **Standards Report** to get a sense of each student's cumulative proficiency in different domains and standards. Check back often to help you anticipate when students need more scaffolding or a challenge.

- Check back in on the **Growth Report** to review students' growth in Lexile® and skills over the course of the year.

Adjust Your Plans Accordingly

Use these data insights to anticipate and adapt instruction, or to assign extra practice. Here are some options:

- Browse the **Text Library** for additional titles at the appropriate Lexile® range. The Lexile® filter can help you narrow results.

- Dig deeper into the **Standards Report** and view aligned resources for each standard. Filter by Component to find the resources that will work for your students.

- Use the **Recommend Groups** functionality to see which students need more instruction or practice with the skills taught in a particular lesson.

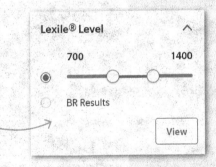

Differentiation

Differentiating Instruction for Students Who Struggle

Identifying the Obstacle

> **What if I don't know exactly what my students are struggling with?**

Tips & Tricks!

Remember that students can excel in one skill set and struggle in another. Rather than labeling students as struggling and successful, try to help each individual draw on strengths and grow where needed.

Use Data, Observation, and Conversation

When students struggle, you'll be better able to help them if you understand their specific obstacles. These tips can help you figure out what those are so you can offer the right support.

- Review the data your district makes available to you.

- **Ed** Analyze the data *Into Literature* provides. If your students have completed the **HMH Growth Measure** and if you've used the learning platform to administer tests, the reports section will be a rich resource. Check the **Standards Report** to see if the student has a pattern of struggling with a particular skill. Use the **Growth Report** to find reading level and proficiency. Both of these reports allow you to compare an individual student's progress to the class average.

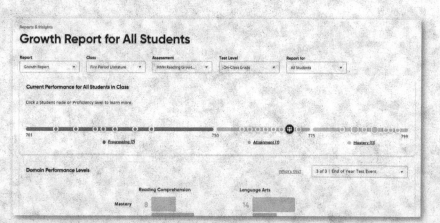

- **Ed** Try assigning a **Guided Skills Practice** that is at or slightly below the student's reading level. Use the Lexile® level filter to find one. If the student can master the skill with an easier text, reading level is likely the biggest obstacle, and you can address that.

- Observe and interact with the student. Are there special needs or social and emotional considerations at play? Students often mask learning struggles with challenges or behavioral issues. Talk to them and get to know them better as people.

- Revisit students' records. If they have an IEP or 504, re-read it. Reach out to the students' teams to discuss what supports are recommended and have worked in the past.

Offering the Right Support

What if students aren't understanding the text?

Tips & Tricks!

While you don't always want to group students by reading level, sometimes it's appropriate. A small group can work together to complete a **Text Sketch** or to read an alternative text. If individual students need resources, provide them discreetly at the beginning of class.

Anticipate and Support

Use the **Lesson Planning Guide** in your Teacher's Edition to identify the text complexity of the selection you plan to teach. If you know it will be a challenge for certain students, be ready to offer appropriate supports.

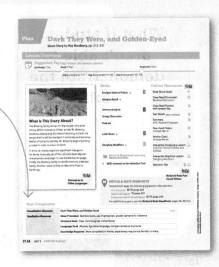

- Use the **Text Support** section of the **Planning Guide** to identify the resources available to you. These might include **Text Sketch**, which provides a high-level visual summary that helps students take notes on key points; **Summary with Targeted Passages**, which provides additional background and easier-to-read summaries of a selection alongside key passages; and **Graphic Organizers** that can help students track events.

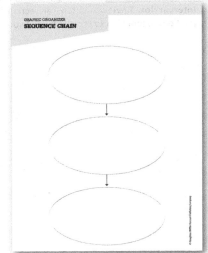

- **Ed** Decide when to offer each resource. If you want students to begin the lesson with these supports, you can print them out or assign them digitally before the class starts to read. If you want students to engage in productive struggle, wait until after they've done a first read.

- **Ed** Suggest that students read along with the audio, which is available with read-along highlighting.

- Refer to the **Differentiated Instruction** notes in the Teacher's Edition that are labeled **When Students Struggle**. These focus on potential points of difficulty and provide strategies for supporting comprehension.

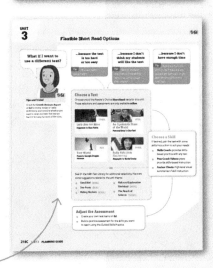

- If you know you have students who won't be able to read the selection even with support, try an alternative text. Refer to the **Flexible Short Read Options** in the **Unit Planning Guides** to see the choices. You can also use the Lexile® filter to browse the **Text Library** for texts at an appropriate level.

What if students aren't able to demonstrate the skill?

Tips & Tricks!

Find these resources on the Ed platform in the **Intervention, Review, & Extension** section. Use the Component filter to search for what you want.

Review and Remediate

HMH surveyed teachers to identify the skills students struggle with most, and *Into Literature* includes a suite of digital resources that provide additional instruction and practice for these concepts.

- Use the **Skills Support** section of the **Planning Guide** to identify the resources available to you.

- Show or assign **Peer Coach Videos.** These short, stand-alone videos explain key skills and can be shown to the whole class, used as part of a station-rotation model, or viewed by individuals who need a refresher and might benefit from hearing a skill explained by someone else.

- Post or distribute **Anchor Charts.** These colorful summaries of the key skills covered by Peer Coach provide a quick reference for students who need reinforcement.

- Assign **Guided Skills Practice**, so students can practice the skills covered by Peer Coach with texts at the appropriate Lexile® range.

- For more robust remediation, assign **Level Up Tutorials.** Follow up with **Level Up Practice Tests**, so students can demonstrate what they've learned and you can collect data on their progress.

- If available in your district, use **Waggle**, HMH's adaptive learning tool, which provides game-like practice in key skills and advances students at their own pace.

Waggle

- Enlist the partnership of parents or guardians and any school or after-school staff who work with the students. These resources can be used at home or as part of additional tutoring and instruction.

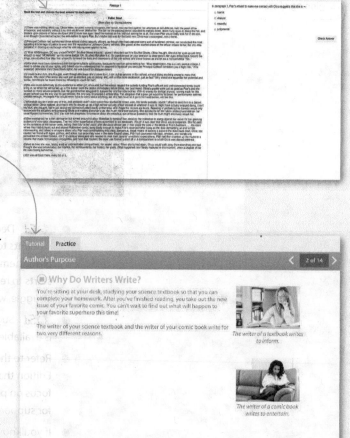

Managing Differentiation in the Classroom

How do I manage having different students doing different things?

Create Effective Groups and Partnerships

Groups will be your friends. Make sure to mix it up, and bring the class together around the essential themes and for moments of fun to create community.

- ☺*Ed* Make targeted assignments. The learning platform allows you to quickly assign appropriate tasks to individuals, groups, or the whole class.

- Group students appropriately. Sometimes, you'll want to group students struggling with the same skill or with the text so that you can give them extra attention while others work more independently. At other times, create mixed groups so that students who have already mastered the skill can provide guidance to those who don't quite get it yet.

- ☺*Ed* Use the **Groups** functionality on the learning platform. Ed uses available data to automatically group students based on assessment performance. This allows you to make group assignments easily. Of course, you can also create your own groups based on your insights or preferences.

- After group work, have students share with the whole class. If students have done different readings, they can report on how each one relates to the unit topic or Essential Question, and a larger discussion can follow from there. If they have worked on skills, they can apply the skill to a text the whole class is familiar with.

- Have "wiggle" breaks of 60 seconds or so to allow students an outlet for their energy. Example: 10 jumping jacks!

- Work in partnership with the students' extended teams, including their grade-level team and their reading coach or other support staff. What struggles transcend your class? What are areas of strength that the students can build from? How can you coordinate your efforts?

- Be mindful that students who struggle will likely not best be helped by additional homework. If you do give practice to be done at home, set clear expectations about time limitations, and keep it under 15 minutes a day.

Supporting English Learners

Planning Your Support

What should I be doing at the beginning of the year?

Prepare Routines and Practices

Start off on a positive note by using these tips.

- 😊**Ed** Review any data you have available about the language proficiency level of the students coming into your classroom.

- Determine an approach with any push-in or pull-out teachers who will be available for additional support.

- Make connections with families, and consider whether there are any school resources that you can use to translate materials you might send home to parents or guardians to keep them informed.

- Consider setting up some one-on-one conferences early on to get to know students and create space for them to communicate any issues they are having. Don't assume they will come to you!

- It can be beneficial to invite students' culture into the classroom, but it's important not to push them or put them on the spot. Gauge their comfort level in one-on-one conversations.

- 😊**Ed** If you have Spanish speakers, review the list of Spanish texts available on the platform and consider incorporating them into your plans. You will find an authentic Spanish text connected to each unit in the middle-school program.

- 😊**Ed** Remember that visual reminders can be extremely helpful. Consider posting anchor charts in the room as you cover texts or skills. On the platform, you will find a selection of anchor charts for key literature skills and Notice & Note signposts.

A leer por tu cuenta

Persistencia

Un cuento de José Bernardo Adolph

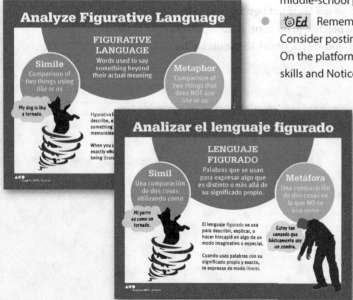

Planning Your Support

> What should
> I be doing at
> the beginning of
> the unit?

**Dark They Were,
and Golden-Eyed**
Science Fiction by **Ray Bradbury**

Close Read Screencast	▶
Text Sketch ENG & SPANISH	📄
Summary with Targeted Passages	📄

| pp. 212–237 | **6** Days | 540L |

Anticipate the Needs of English Learners

Access planning guides and support resources to meet the needs of all your students.

- Preview the **Unit Planning Guides** to get an overview of texts included in the unit. Note any with a Lexile® level that might challenge your students. Note selections that include **Text Sketch** and **Summaries and Adapted Texts**.

- *Ed* Access **Spanish Unit Resources** in the Reading Resources category on the platform to find Spanish-language versions of each unit's description and theme, the Response Log, and academic vocabulary.

- *Ed* Consult the **Multilingual Glossary** to locate any terms for which you want to include additional support in your plan. This resource can be found in the Reading Resources category on the platform and includes a glossary of literary and informational terms, academic vocabulary, and critical vocabulary in ten languages: Spanish, Haitian-Creole, Portuguese, Vietnamese, French, Arabic, Chinese, Russian, Tagalog, and Urdu.

Glossary of Literary and Informational Terms

English	Spanish
Act An act is a major division within a play, similar to a chapter in a book. Each act may be further divided into smaller sections, called scenes. Plays can have as many as five acts, or as few as one.	**Acto** Un acto es una división importante dentro de una obra, similar a un capítulo en un libro. Cada acto, a su vez, se puede dividir en secciones más pequeñas, denominadas escenas. Las obras pueden tener hasta cinco actos, o solo uno.
Alliteration Alliteration is the repetition of consonant sounds at the beginning of words. Note the repetition of the *d* sound in this line: The *d*aring boy *d*ove into the *d*eep sea.	**Aliteración** Aliteración es la reiteración de sonidos consonantes al comienzo de las palabras. Observe la repetición del sonido *d* en esta oración en idioma inglés: The *d*aring boy *d*ove into the *d*eep sea.
Allusion An allusion is a reference to a famous person, place, event, or work of literature.	**Alusión** Una alusión es una referencia a una persona, un lugar, un acontecimiento o una obra literaria conocidos.

- Incorporate time into your plans to help English learners build background and context for the texts.

- Keep lines of communication open with any push-in or pull-out teachers who may also be supporting these students, so you can align your goals and share resources.

How can I support English learners with *Into Literature* texts?

Tips & Tricks!

Infuse your lesson plans with cooperative learning activities to promote oral language development, grouping students with mixed language proficiency levels. You can use the grouping functionality on the HMH platform to create and manage groups.

Choose the Right Support for Each Text

Into Literature includes a wide selection of support for English learners. Pick and choose what works best for your students.

- ⊙Ed Before you introduce any text, use the **Multilingual Glossary** to create a personal word list in the student's native language, or assign it as an activity for students.

- ⊙Ed Assign or print **Summaries in Multiple Languages** in English and the student's native language, and bundle them with the following resources to make sure students have a basic understanding of the key ideas, events, and characters in the text:

  - **Summaries and Adapted Texts:** select texts in an adapted format with targeted passages to support less-proficient readers
  - **Text Sketch (in English and in Spanish):** high-level visual summaries of a selection

- ⊙Ed Have students use the audio in the eBook to assist with comprehension. They can also turn on the **Read-Along Highlight** feature to track the text as the audio is read.

- Use the Teacher's Edition **Lesson Planning Guides** to find information about the text complexity of each selection and to survey detailed support for that lesson in the **For English Learners** feature, including tips for building background, cultural notes, language objectives, and a list of additional online resources.

- The Teacher's Edition also includes point-of-use **Scaffolding for English Learners** notes to support the teaching of each text.

- Use the oral assessment questions provided with the **Assessment Practice** in each lesson of the Teacher's Edition.

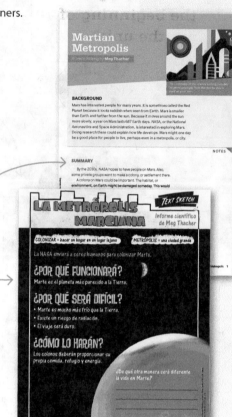

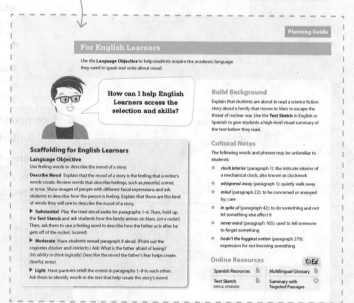

Text Support for English Learners

How can I support English learners with *any* grade-level text I teach?

ⓔ**Ed**

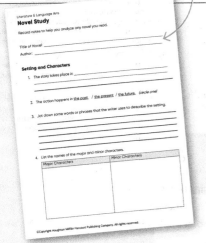

Use Sentence Frames

Sentence frames are a helpful tool to scaffold English learners; such frames allow students to think about what they want to say without the distraction of how to phrase their response. Here are some sentence frames you might use to help English learners analyze and appreciate different genres.

Fiction

- The story takes place in…
- The story is told from the…point of view.
- Three words that describe the main character are…
- The main problem in the story is…
- The author communicates an important message about…
- I would/would not recommend this story to a friend because…

Nonfiction

- The main idea is…
- Three details that support the main idea are…
- In this paragraph, the author is saying…
- The author includes this section because…
- The author wrote this because he or she wanted to…
- I agree/disagree with the author about…because…

Poetry

- The poem is mostly about…
- Three details about the poem's form are…
- One thing I noticed about the speaker of the poem is…
- Three words or phrases that really stand out to me are…
- One tool the poet uses is… to communicate…
- The poem communicates an important message about…using these details:…

ⓔ**Ed**

Add Skills Support

For additional skills support, you can pair any text with the following *Into Literature* resources.

- **Peer Coach Videos:** videos of students' peers teaching skills
- **Anchor Charts (in English and Spanish):** high-level visual summaries of skills and ideas
- **Level Up Tutorials:** skills-based remediation lessons for students
- **Skills Coach:** skills instruction and activities that can be applied to any text

Infusing Rigor and Challenge

Meeting the Needs of All Students

How can I meet the needs of my more advanced students?

Discover Challenge and Rigor at Your Fingertips

Students come into your class with a wide range of experiences and ability levels. As a teacher, you likely spend a lot of time working to get struggling students up to level. But what about students who need a little more rigor and more challenge? With its balanced approach, *Into Literature* has options for your classroom that will allow you infuse rigor and challenges into all of your lessons.

With *Into Literature*, you will find:

- **Rigorous texts:** Our cross-genre units contain a mixture of accessible and challenging texts. You will find short and accessible texts that ease students into the themes and topics, but you will also find classic and complex texts that will push students. To help you decide which texts to teach in a given unit, consult your Teacher's Edition **Lesson Planning Guides** for information about the complexity of each text.

- **Rigorous analysis:** Rich, complex texts are at the heart of *Into Literature*. The instruction and activities all focus on the text. Students are given ample opportunities to make personal connections and to engage in creative work, but they are consistently asked to return to the text for close analysis and study. You can use the **Analyze the Text** questions after each selection to sharpen students' critical thinking, analysis, and synthesis skills. Look in your Teacher's Edition for information about the Depth of Knowledge (DOK) level of each question.

- **Rigorous assignments:** Sometimes, all you need is a short ten-minute assignment to quickly check in on your students. But to get a better sense of how they're performing, you need longer, more complex assignments. The **Choices** activities following each text, as well as the cumulative tasks at the end of each unit, offer opportunities to challenge your students.

Consider Your Sources

Review the list of texts in the unit and choose at least two that you may want to use as sources of ideas for your literary analysis.

As you review potential sources, consult the notes you made on your **Response Log** and make additional notes about any ideas that might be useful as you write your analysis. Include source titles and page numbers in your notes to help you provide accurate text evidence and citations when you include support from these texts.

UNIT 2 SOURCES

- [ ] What Is the Horror Genre?
- [ ] The Tell-Tale Heart
- [ ] The Monkey's Paw
- [ ] *from* The Monkey's Paw MEDIA
- [ ] *from* The Aeneid of Virgil
- [ ] *from* Hades: Lord of the Dead

Possible responses:

(1) **DOK 2:** *Mars is the most Earthlike planet.*

(2) **DOK 2:** *The author uses a compare-contrast structure to compare Mars with Earth.*

(3) **DOK 3:** *Mars has metal and rock. Settlers could use local dirt to make bricks to build houses. They could use silicon and iron to produce glass and steel for a number of structures, including greenhouses that can be used to grow food. They could use solar energy to produce heat and electricity, and carbon dioxide from the Martian atmosphere to produce methane for fuel for trips to Earth.*

(4) **DOK 3:** *The author uses a problem-solution structure in this section to help develop the idea that settling Mars can and should be done. The problem-solution structure explains how settlers could overcome obstacles and problems with the Martian environment to create a habitable settlement.*

(5) **DOK 4:** *The numbers and stats help support the idea that building a colony on Mars will be challenging but possible.*

(6) **DOK 4:** *Settlers would have a mostly vegan diet because they would be consuming mostly plant-based foods that they might grow on Mars. Students might cite the word colony as one they figured out, based on the word habitat and the last line of the paragraph.*

Meeting the Needs of All Students

How can I go beyond just giving students extra work?

Find Flexible Options That Go Beyond Extra Work

Some of your students aren't struggling with on-level work. One of the easiest things to do for those students is to give them … more work. But what if you want to give them different texts or tasks to work on—ones that will challenge them or push them to develop new and useful skills?

Into Literature contains a varied set of extension activities that will help you get beyond handing out extra work.

- **Leveled Texts Library:** Choose from a diverse set of selections that range from easy to very hard. You can choose the selections that you know will appeal to students or choose from the suggested unit-level connections to stay focused on the unit assignments.

- **Novels:** There are lots of ways to incorporate longer texts in your classroom: whole-class instruction, literature circles, or independent work. But however you incorporate them, HMH has a varied set of options to choose from, including classic and contemporary works and texts that will speak to a broad range of experiences and backgrounds. Consult the **Flexible Long Reads** section of the **Unit Planning Guides** in your Teacher's Edition to help you choose appropriate novels for those students who need a challenge. You might also assign some of the **Choices** prompts and activities in the **HMH Study Guides** for these titles.

As Usual
Short story by Jessica Wilkening-Hayes

Esports ARE Sports!

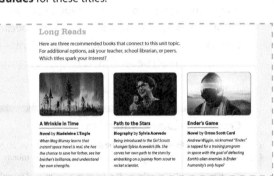

Long Reads

Here are three recommended books that connect to this unit topic.
For additional options, ask your teacher, school librarian, or peers.
Which titles spark your interest?

A Wrinkle in Time
Novel by Madeleine L'Engle
When Meg Murray learns that instant space travel is real, she has the chance to save her father, see her brother's brilliance, and understand her own strengths.

Path to the Stars
Biography by Sylvia Acevedo
Being introduced to the Girl Scouts changes Sylvia Acevedo's life. She carves her own path to the stars by embarking on a journey from scout to rocket scientist.

Ender's Game
Novel by Orson Scott Card
Andrew Wiggin, nicknamed "Ender," is tapped for a training program in space with the goal of defeating Earth's alien enemies. Is Ender humanity's only hope?

- **Independent Reading:** You do a lot of reading with your students. But we all know that the ultimate goal is for students to read with independence, without scaffolds and supports, at the appropriate Lexile® level. The **Reader's Choice** strand is designed to match students with the right texts, including high-complexity options.

- **Media Projects:** Some students need something totally different. How about responding to the unit by writing a song? Or creating a comic strip? Or producing a documentary? Every unit in the program has a suggested **Media Project** for you to choose from, to stretch students or to let them show their creative side. You can find instruction and support for each activity online.

What guidance is there in the Teacher's Edition on rigor and challenge?

Find Ample Support for Stretching Your Students

When you're planning your lessons, one of the many things you're thinking about is the level of rigor you want and how to plan for all of your students, including those above level. Your *Into Literature* Teacher's Edition gives you planning support and point-of-use suggestions that you need.

● **Text Complexity:** You know that text complexity is a complicated thing. Having a Lexile® score is always helpful, but it's impossible to boil the complexity of a text down to a number. That's why every selection contains a full Text Complexity rubric, focusing on what, specifically, makes this text more or less complex.

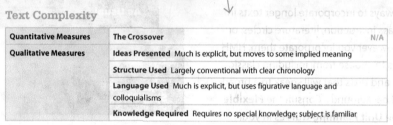

Text Complexity		
Quantitative Measures	The Crossover	N/A
Qualitative Measures	**Ideas Presented** Much is explicit, but moves to some implied meaning	
	Structure Used Largely conventional with clear chronology	
	Language Used Much is explicit, but uses figurative language and colloquialisms	
	Knowledge Required Requires no special knowledge; subject is familiar	

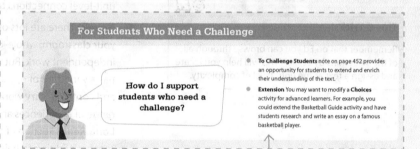

How do I support students who need a challenge?

For Students Who Need a Challenge

● **To Challenge Students** note on page 452 provides an opportunity for students to extend and enrich their understanding of the text.

● **Extension** You may want to modify a **Choices** activity for advanced learners. For example, you could extend the Basketball Guide activity and have students research and write an essay on a famous basketball player.

● **Challenging Students:** Every selection in the program contains a planning note (**For Students Who Need a Challenge**) that highlights point-of-use suggestions on what you can do to keep advanced students engaged and developing. It also highlights specific aspects of the lesson that might be well suited for advanced students—for example, a **Choices** activity that might be something to steer advanced students toward.

Cross-Curricular Connection

Compare Benefits of Sports and the Arts Tell students that "It's Not Just a Game!" details ways in which sports benefit us as individuals and as a community.

● Have students think about other types of activities that provide pleasure as well as social benefits.

● As students read, ask them to compare ways in which participation in sports and other activities such as theater, art, and music can help strengthen communities and enhance citizenship, leadership, and global thinking.

● **Cross-Curricular Resources:** At point of use, you will find suggested **Cross-Curricular Connections**. Reaching across the curriculum to deepen and broaden your students' knowledge is a great way to infuse your classroom with rigor.

Extending Students' Learning

Beyond the text sets in the program, what other resources does *Into Literature* have for me to use?

Go Beyond the Textbook

Much of the focus of *Into Literature* is on the selections and the support for those selections. In addition, the program offers other engaging and flexible resources you can use to make sure that students are reaching their potential.

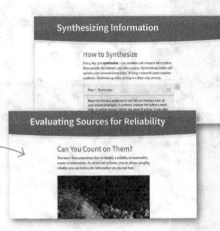

- **Interactive Lessons:** On Ed you will find a diverse set of stand-alone lessons on Grammar, Writing, Speaking and Listening, and Vocabulary that you can assign based on the needs of your students. For example, if you have students who want to dig deeper into a writing concept, such as incorporating textual evidence in more sophisticated and varied ways, you can assign them more detailed and granular lessons to get them to the next level.

- Writable Browse **Writable**'s extensive library for prompts and assignments that you can use to extend students' learning. You might search by skill if you want to provide more practice in a targeted area, or use the rubrics and resources within Writable to create your own assignments.

- **Current Events:** There a world outside your classroom, and bringing that world into your daily lessons is a great way to expand and deepen your students' understanding. Through Ed, you have access to curated Current Events links that are timely, sophisticated, and safe for your classroom.

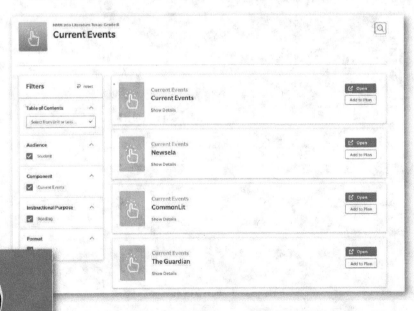

- **Peer Coach Videos:** *Into Literature* provides a library of videos in which students' peers teach them more about key skills, such as citing text evidence and analyzing themes. How about stretching your students and having them create peer coach videos of their own? Encourage them to choose skills in which they are "experts."

Purposeful Technology

Getting the Most Out of Ed: Your Friend in Learning

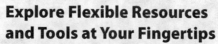

Getting Acquainted with Ed

What does the platform offer me?

Tips & Tricks!

New to *Into Literature*? No worries! Start your orientation of the program by exploring the **Professional Learning** section of Ed.

Explore Flexible Resources and Tools at Your Fingertips

Use the HMH learning platform to view the *Into Literature* scope and sequence for your grade level, dip into flexible resources, curate your own lesson plans, create assignments and groups, and monitor student progress.

Into Literature Digital Units and Lessons

- Six thematic units cover a range of grade-appropriate topics and pair high-interest texts with the ELA skills your students need to learn, practice, and progress as readers and writers.

- Access countless resources to create units, lessons, or individual assignments that meet your learning goals.

And So Much More...

- Log in and check your dashboard at least once a week. This will give you an overview of any assignments you need to review, announcements about platform updates, and other helpful messages.

- Track assignments (for the whole class, small groups, or individuals) and monitor students' progress.

- Review assessment results and track student proficiency and growth.

- Create and manage small groups, and easily assign resources to your groups.

- Create your own lesson plans.

- Create custom assessments and test items.

- Find an ever-growing library of professional learning resources from authentic classroom videos, to tips from other teachers and our team of experienced coaches, to support for implementing *Into Literature*.

Available Resources

There are a variety of resource types available for you to use.

- **eBook:** Interactive digital content that launches in the HMH digital reader, and includes read-along audio and highlighting for text selections, annotation tools, **Teacher Review** functionality, and ability to assign to Google® Classroom

- **PDF:** Downloadable and printable resources

- **Digital Assessment:** Diagnostic, formative, and summative tests with interactive items; student assessment data collected and displayed in reports

- **Editable File:** Downloadable, editable, and printable resources

- **Video:** Brief videos for a variety of instructional purposes

- **External Links:** Links to age-appropriate and relevant content, such as current events, that relates to *Into Literature* units

How do I find what I'm looking for?

Ed

Tips & Tricks!

Whether you are browsing lesson lists, standards, or search results, you can use filters to help narrow the results.

Try Five Ways to Locate Resources

Depending on what you are seeking, there are many ways to find the resources you need on the HMH learning platform.

1. Browse the units and lessons in the unit carousel. Select a unit and browse through its various lessons. Click on a lesson to see a list of all the resources related to that lesson.

2. Use these resource categories to browse different resource types.

3. You can also browse by standards. Select the standard you're interested in to see a list of all of the resources associated with that standard.

4. If you are looking for something specific, you can search by keyword.

5. To find what you're looking for, refer to the **Resource Overview**, which is located in the Program Overview category on the platform. Keep in mind that the content on Ed is always evolving—in response to feedback from users like you! Check the Help section to learn about the latest ways to browse and explore resources.

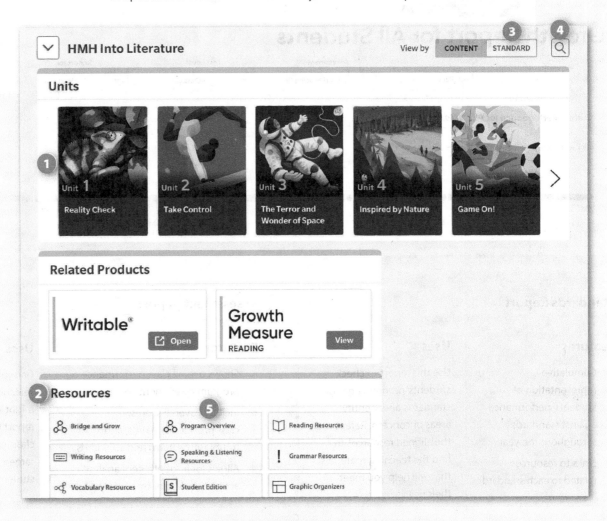

Let the Data Guide Your Choices

Data and reports can help you monitor students' progress and make teaching decisions that support the needs of all your students.

What do I do with all these reports?

Growth Report

Features

- Administer the **HMH Growth Measure** three times a year: beginning, midpoint, and end

- Use the results to identify each student's Lexile® range, proficiency in reading comprehension and language domains, and growth across various increments of the year

Uses

Use this report to identify students at risk, and to benchmark their performance. You can also use the Lexile® scores to help you gauge when a text will be too hard or too easy for your class and to differentiate.

Growth Report for All Students

Report	Class	Assessment	Test Level	Report for
Growth Report	First Period Literature	HMH Reading Growt...	On-Class Grade	All Students

Current Performance for All Students in Class

Click a Student node or Proficiency level to learn more.

701   750   775   799

● Progressing (7)   ● Attainment (7)   ● Mastery (11)

Standards Report

Features

- Cumulative representation of students' performance against standards throughout the year

- Links to resources related to each standard

Uses

Use this report to check students' progress against standards and identify areas of concern. Refer to the aligned resources to find the teaching materials that will help you meet their needs.

Assessment Report

Features

- Shows overall class performance on program assessments

- Includes overall scores, class proficiency bands, and troublesome items and standards

- Allows for in-depth item analysis across the class or by student

Uses

Gauge how students performed on the selection or unit and identify skills you might want to reteach. Pivot from this report to planning your next whole-class lesson or unit, or plan some targeted differentiation for individual students or groups.

Making Ed Work for You

What if I don't want to teach what you've suggested?

Tips & Tricks!

Not only can you create your own lesson plans; you can also use the HMH platform to share them with your fellow teachers.

Make It Your Own

Into Literature was created with your need for flexibility in mind. Whether you want to adapt the scope and sequence, or start from scratch and create your own curriculum, or anything in between, HMH has got you covered.

Fine-Tuning

- If you are looking to fine-tune a lesson we have provided, begin by creating your own lesson plan on the platform.

- Select the unit and lesson you'd like to fine tune from the program carousel. Preview the resources included with this lesson—you might start with the **Lesson Planning Guide** in the Teacher's Edition so you can scan our suggested approach.

- As you make decisions about which portions of the lesson to include, add them to your custom lesson plan. For example, you may decide not to teach the language convention skill we've paired with the text, so you can omit those related resources from your plan.

- You can browse across all the *Into Literature* resources and add additional supporting resources to meet different learning goals. For example, you might decide to replace our suggested literary skill with a different one. In this case, you may choose to add a **Peer Coach Video**, **Anchor Chart**, and **Skills Coach** for the skill you have selected. As you find additional resources, add them to your custom plan.

Starting From Scratch

- If you are looking to create your own lesson from scratch, begin by creating your own lesson plan on the platform.

- If you have hyperlinks to external resources, you can include them in the **Plan Description.**

- Browse for the resources you'd like to use to build your lesson.

- As you find resources you'd like to include, add them to your plan.

Is it worth it to assign the readings digitally?

Decide for Yourself!

This is a matter of personal preference and depends on how you like to manage your classroom and homework assignments, but there are some benefits to assigning readings digitally:

● When reading an HMH eBook in our digital reader, students can access the read-aloud selection audio and hear the text read aloud to them. The digital reader also includes a read-along highlighting feature, which highlights the text as it is read aloud so students can easily follow along with the audio.

● As they read, students can annotate the text digitally, and you can review their annotations from your own copy of the digital assignment by using the **Teacher Review** functionality.

● Working in the digital text allows you to easily present the text to the whole class for discussion purposes, and display either your own text annotations or samples of students' annotations.

Tips & Tricks!

Students can download an app to access digital readings offline anytime, anywhere.

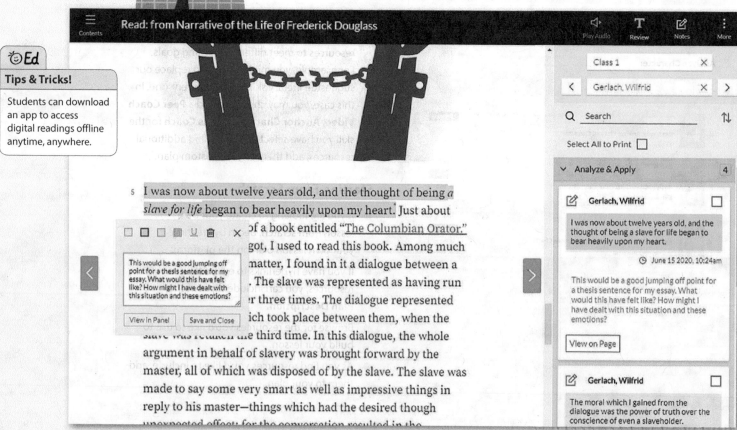

Making Ed Work for You

> ### How will I review students' digital work?

Use Assignments, Teacher Review, and Reports

Ed offers a variety of ways to monitor students' work and progress, depending on the kind of assignment you have created.

- Review your assignments in the Assignment List, and track students' progress. From this list, selecting an eBook assignment or assessment will allow you to launch and review students' work.

- Launch eBook assignments in the HMH digital reader to review how students have interacted with the text. Select the **Teacher Review** functionality from the top navigation bar and select students whose work you'd like to review. You can also use the feedback icon on the eBook page to leave feedback for students.

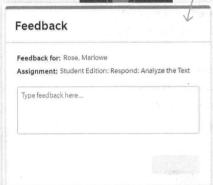

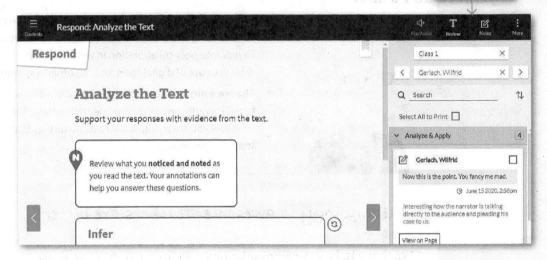

- If you have created online writing assignments, you can easily review students' writing progress, scan peer feedback, and provide feedback of your own.

- Use the reports on Ed to monitor progress on assessments.

> ### I'm not a fan of technology. What if I don't want to use the platform?

Use Our Printable Resources

If you prefer to assign and manage student work in the physical world, you can limit your platform use to locating resources—there is so much to print out!

- Any of our PDF resources can be easily printed. They include a variety of practice activities, graphic organizers, and text and skills support.

- Use the **Text Library** to find printable texts across genres and Lexile® levels.

- If you prefer not to assign digital assessments, you can print out **Selection Tests** and **Unit Tests** and have students respond on paper.

Integrating Technology into the ELA Classroom

Getting Started

> I want to use technology in my instruction. Where do I start?

Start With Your Learning Objectives

HMH Into Literature consultant Weston Kieschnick acknowledges that we've collectively gotten caught up in buzzwords and technology tools at the expense of purposeful pedagogy and instruction. When it comes to successfully implementing technology in your classroom, begin with the basics—what you want your students to achieve.

- **Reflect on and outline your instructional objectives.** Is it your goal to model close reading and annotation? To determine which students need more support? To promote peer collaboration in writing and revision? Let your learning objectives drive your use of digital tools, not the other way around.

- **Choose a digital tool.** From polling software to vocabulary game applications to collaborative writing and presentation tools, there are just-right tools for whatever you are trying to do. Look no further than the pages in this article for some suggestions.

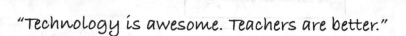

"Technology is awesome. Teachers are better."

"We have to layer technologies onto our instruction ... we must do so with strategy, pedagogy, and purpose. That comes from educators, not from the technologies themselves."

— from *Bold School: Old School Wisdom + New School Technologies*

Weston Kieschnick

- **Lean on the support and guidance of fellow educators.** Remember that you are not in this alone. Pose questions on social media or in your professional learning community and you'll soon see the tips and guidance pour in. Enlist the support and advice of your school technology coordinator, and be open to experimenting with new ideas and approaches. Don't be afraid to embrace them! Even if a new tool turns out to be an "epic fail," it's still a learning opportunity.

Enhancing Whole-Class Instruction

How might I use technology in whole-class instruction?

Consider the Options

Technology can ignite your whole-class instruction, as well as adding interest and variety to your lessons. Depending on your instructional objectives, here are some ideas you might consider.

If you want to...   *Try This!*   *Using These Tools*

 Generate Class Discussion

Create a digital poll that invites students to share their opinions about an Essential Question or an argument. (Example: Is space exploration a daring adventure or a dangerous risk?) Use the results to guide a meaningful class discussion at the beginning of a unit.

- *Google® Forms*
- *SurveyMonkey®*

 Gauge Understanding or Mastery

A three-question **Assessment Practice** follows each text in *Into Literature*. While you can assign this resource as independent practice on our platform, you also might consider using a whole-class quiz site to quickly learn which students did not comprehend the main ideas.

- *Quizlet®*
- *Google® Forms*

 Expand Students' Vocabulary

Incite friendly competition among students by creating a game that tests their knowledge of unit academic and lesson vocabulary words.

- *KAHOOT!®*
- *Vocabulary.com*
- *Gimkit*

😊 Ed

Tips & Tricks!

Have students annotate the text as homework or independent practice. Then, use the Teacher Review function in your eBook to project students' annotations in your next day's lesson.

 Model Close Reading

Project the teacher's version of the **Student eBook** and use the highlighter and notes to annotate the text and answer questions. Thinking aloud about the process of close reading can help your students see how it's done.

- *Student eBook on 😊 Ed*

 Allow More Class Time for Meaningful Discussion, Group Work, or Writing

Try a blended-learning approach to maximize valuable class time. Create a video or screen capture of yourself delivering instruction and have students review that lesson at home. Use class time for discussion, questions, and small-group differentiation.

- *Apple QuickTime*
- *Screencastify*

 Increase Student Autonomy

Challenge your students to be teachers for a day! Invite groups of students to instruct the rest of the class in a particular skill. Allow students to use presentation software to illustrate or emphasize key points.

- *Microsoft PowerPoint*
- *NearPod*
- *Google® Slides*

How can I use technology in small-group and independent work?

Have a Plan

If you establish a plan and set up your classroom ahead of time, you can use technology in instructionally meaningful ways to support small-group and independent practice. This allows you to spend your time differentiating instruction for those students who need it most.

Implement these ideas to keep the rest of the class on track.

Use Station Rotations

● **To Reinforce Skills** Have groups of students review a **Peer Coach** video and accompanying **Anchor Chart** for a particular skill you've taught recently. To practice the skill, you might have the group work through a **Level Up Tutorial**.

● **To Inspire Signpost Discussions** Assign small groups of students to read a text of their choosing and ask them to look for Notice & Note signposts. Encourage them to use their eBook annotation tools to highlight and identify those signposts, as well as to discuss the anchor question.

Assign Independent Practice

● **For More Skills Application** Assign **Guided Skills Practice** for on-level skills practice. Use **Waggle** for practice geared toward those students who may need more support.

● **For Reading Support** Have students listen to the read-aloud of a particular text. You may want to encourage them to turn on **Read-Along Highlighting** so that they can better follow along.

● **For Improving Writing** Use the Peer Review feature in **Writable** to inspire collaboration and revision in your classroom. Set it up so that each student reviews the work of two or three classmates.

Waggle

Writable

Create Project-Based Learning Opportunities

Use the **Media Projects** at the end of each unit to kickstart small-group project-based learning. From Google® Slides to Nearpod to GarageBand to iMovie, there is no shortage of digital tools to inspire students' creativity. Encourage groups to start low-tech or no-tech: planning and storyboarding are even more important than the final product.

Create a Movie Trailer

This unit includes stories from all over the world. Choose one of them and create a trailer for a movie adaptation of the story. Your trailer should include onscreen text, images, and music. Make sure your trailer hints at the story's theme and makes viewers want to know more.

Now Go Create!

> **How do I set up my class for successful distance learning?**

Stay Connected

If recent events have taught us anything, it's that sometimes we have to be ready to teach and learn at a distance. Yet, with a little preparation, patience, and perseverance, we can use technology to keep classrooms connected. These tips can help with virtual routines.

Get Ready for Your Close-Ups

- Remote learning can be isolating for educators and students alike. Maintain your connections via video. Video-conferencing applications like Google® Hangouts, Microsoft Teams, and Zoom® can help to cultivate a classroom community. Use the **Virtual Classroom** function on our platform to manage your classroom collaboration.

- Work with your administration on the setup and logistics, and then experiment with the application prior to use. Consider doing a dry run with a colleague before showtime!

- If you don't have video conferencing as an option, record and post a video of yourself each day. You might preview the day's assignments or deliver a short lesson.

- Not all students will have access. Ensure that video sessions are optional, and make an extra effort to follow up—either by email or telephone—with those students who can't connect. Take advantage of the offline app so that students can access *Into Literature* digital resources without an Internet connection.

Balance Real-Time Teaching with Independent Work

- Strive for real-time learning each day even for a short time. You might review vocabulary or literary and informational text terms using some of the game applications on page 121. Another option is to model close reading of part of a text before having students complete the reading independently. Hold a class discussion about the rest of the text in a subsequent video session.

- Assign independent reading each day, having students use the read-along highlighting function in their eBooks.

- Browse through the digital lessons on writing, speaking and listening, vocabulary, and grammar, which are perfect for self-guided independent work.

- Consider having students post a video doing a close-reading of an excerpt from a text. Students can consult the **Close Read Screencasts** as models and use screen-capture software to produce their final product.

Communicate Regularly

- Let students and parents know that you are available by email or chat during school hours each day.

- Consider hosting office hours for parents each week. Remember—most parents are not experts at supervising learning at home and may appreciate your tips and tricks. Your reassurance may just assuage some anxiety at home!

Promoting Digital Literacy

Understanding the Basics

What is digital literacy and why does it matter?

Tips & Tricks!

With your students, generate a list of media messages they are exposed to, such as the ones shown on the sticky notes. Ask: How does each message affect or influence you?

Create Critical Thinkers, Consumers, and Citizens

Never have we had more information and entertainment at our fingertips.

● Social-media influencers feature brands and products in their videos. We are subtly persuaded to buy.

● The 24/7 news cycle captures our attention with the latest headlines and commentary. That news shapes our perceptions of the world.

● Movie studios release their latest films, hoping for box-office blockbusters. We flock to the theaters to escape reality and be entertained.

John Naisbitt, who co-wrote the now decades-old book *Megatrends*, said that "We are drowning in information but starved for knowledge." Never has this statement been truer than in today's world. The *quantity* of information has exploded because anyone can publish content. Yet, in some cases, *quality* has diminished, With fewer checks and balances on that content, it's hard for us to know what to believe, whom to trust, and how such media messages affect our purchasing decisions, political opinions, beliefs, and perceptions.

This is a strong case for **media literacy**—the ability to read, analyze, evaluate, and think critically about the media messages students are exposed to each day. Media literacy also involves students' ability to produce messages for specific purposes and audiences, using the techniques they've learned about in their analysis. Media-literacy education belongs in the ELA classroom.

Types of Media Messages

Documentaries
Commercials
Social Networking Sites
Movies
TV Shows
Online Chat Forums
Memes
Magazines
Infomercials
Political Ads
Billboards
Internet Ads
Newspapers
Web News
Radio Programming
Infographics
Music
Giphy Art
Podcasts
Interactive Games
Apps
Product Packaging
Brochures
Blogs

Exploring Key Questions

How can I help students analyze media messages?

Introduce and Discuss Five Questions

Leaders in media-literacy education agree on five key questions for analyzing any media message, be it a political ad, social-networking site, commercial, movie, or news blog. At the beginning of the year, introduce these questions to your students, using the information in the chart. Revisit these questions throughout the year as part of any media lesson you use in specific units of study.

Five Key Questions	Why They're Important
1 Who created this message?	Media messages can come from a variety of sources—for example, individuals spouting strong opinions, companies selling products, or filmmakers weaving imaginative stories. Identifying the creator of a media message is the first step in understanding its purpose and techniques.
2 What techniques are used to grab and hold my attention?	Bold colors and eye-catching logos can emphasize key benefits of a product. Lighting, sound effects, and editing can draw us into a suspenseful movie scene. Sensational headlines can skew our understanding of an unfolding news story. Analyzing these techniques can make us more aware of how they affect our decisions, actions, and perceptions.
3 How might different people understand this message differently?	No two people will experience a media message the same way. That's because age, gender, values, lifestyle, and opinions influence what people see and hear. For instance, a victim of identity theft will have a different reaction to a movie about the topic than someone who has never experienced it firsthand. When analyzing any media message, consider how your own experiences are influencing you and think about how others might respond.
4 What values, lifestyles, and points of view are reflected in—or omitted from—this message?	All media messages are constructed. Just as creators make choices about information to include and techniques to use, they are just as deliberate about what to leave out. Through these choices, creators transmit particular viewpoints and values. Ask: What ideas are being "sold"? What values and behaviors are portrayed in a positive light? In a negative light? Consider the ways in which the media message influences your worldview.
5 Why is this message being sent?	In simplistic terms, the purpose of any media message is to inform, entertain, and/or persuade. Yet, it's important for audiences to uncover deeper motives. Most media messages are created to gain profit or power. Behind every amusing social-media influencer video are sponsors who have paid to feature their products there. Behind every blockbuster film are movie-studio executives hoping for record ticket sales. Consider both overt and subtle purposes when examining any message.

> How can I incorporate media analysis into the study of literature?

Visual elements include the images, the style of the images, and the ways in which the elements work together.

ANIMATION	images that appear to move; created through drawings, computer graphics, or photographs
FILM FOOTAGE	visual images captured on film or digitally; edited to deliver information clearly
GRAPHICS	drawings (maps, charts, diagrams, and so on) used to represent ideas or data

Sound elements include what you hear in a video.

MUSIC	instrumental and/or singing; emphasizes the emotional mood; may signal shifts in topic
NARRATION	words spoken over the images; carefully worded to present key facts

Help Students "Read" Media Messages

Like novels, short stories, and nonfiction, media messages are texts worthy of careful study and analysis. Whereas writers employ techniques like foreshadowing, figurative language, and rhetorical devices to craft their texts, media creators use techniques of their own to influence audiences.

The English language arts classroom is the perfect place to make a natural connection between writers' and media creators' crafts. Here are some suggestions you might try.

- **Include media texts in your units of study.** The *Into Literature* Student Edition includes media texts—such as graphic novels, posters, videos, screenplays, and documentaries—embedded within certain units. Take advantage of these built-in opportunities for media analysis.

- **Encourage close viewing.** Like written texts, media texts require multiple viewings. If you are watching something as a class, encourage students to view it first for comprehension and enjoyment. Then watch the clip a second time, pausing periodically to ask questions, discuss techniques, and think critically about purpose and audience.

- **Teach visual techniques.** Different **camera shots** can establish setting, provide key details, or reveal emotion. **Editing** techniques can create fast-paced suspense or communicate a more relaxed mood. **Type**, **font**, and **composition** can convey meaning in each frame of a graphic novel. Make sure students understand the varied visual techniques that media creators have at their disposal. Use the media lessons in the Student Edition to bolster your instruction.

- **Analyze the influence of sound.** Voice-over narration can communicate information and establish a tone of authority in news reports and documentaries. **Music** and **sound effects** can create a mood or influence an audience's emotions. When students "read" media messages, prompt them to consider the effects of specific sounds.

- **Revisit the five questions.** With any media message you teach, refer back to the five questions on the previous page. You'll notice that your students will start to think more critically about what they see and hear through frequent discussions about these questions.

Monster!
The Story of My Miserable Life

Starring
Steve Harmon

Produced by
Steve Harmon

Directed by
Steve Harmon

(Credits continue to roll.)

The incredible story of how one guy's life was turned around by a few events

Evaluating Sources

> **What are the best ways to teach students to evaluate sources?**

Provide Ample Practice

Anyone with media-production skills and inexpensive applications can create content and make it available on the Web for mass consumption. Sometimes, the polish and production value of those sources of content can mask inaccuracies and biases. Being able to evaluate sources critically is an essential skill for college, careers, and, well, life in general! Use these tips to help students practice this essential skill.

- Use the **Interactive Writing Lessons** on evaluating sources to cover the basics as a whole class. For application, look for research-based **Choices** activities following each lesson.

- Make good use of the end-of-unit writing task focused on research. Consider using **Writable** so that students can complete their drafts digitally and take advantage of tools like peer review.

- Check out the **Current Events** category on Ed, which includes access to HMH's own frequently updated site. Browse for up-to-the-minute articles that you might assign to give students practice in evaluating sources.

Creating a Culture of Media Makers

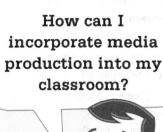

> **How can I incorporate media production into my classroom?**

Make the Time for Media Production

Production is a necessary aspect of media-literacy education. It deserves class time in proportion to its instructional weight. Consider these ideas and resources as you work to unleash students' inner creativity.

- Consult the **Choices** feature after each lesson for activities focused on media production.

- **Ed** Try out project-based learning! Explore the end-of-unit **Media Projects** on Ed and think about allowing students to demonstrate their knowledge of at least one unit by completing one of these projects.

- Hold a student showcase. Build in time for students to share their final products with the rest of the class.

- Encourage reflection. After each project, ask: What are you most proud of? What would you do differently next time? What was your group's biggest challenge?

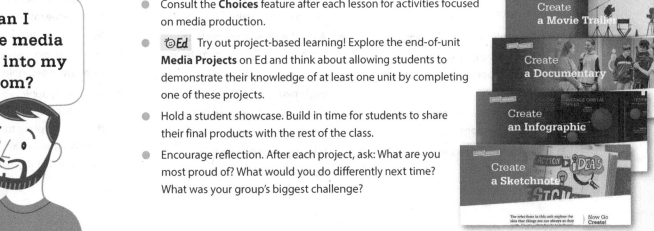

Making the Most of an Accessible Learning Experience

Understanding the Basics

Level the Playing Field for Learning

Accessibility is about the right to *equity* for the disabled. Federal law calls for all public schools to offer equity in education to every student they serve. So, providers of instructional materials strive to produce print and digital learning experiences that are usable by all students, regardless of disability.

But approaching something as many-sided as equity in education takes more than minimum compliance to the law or to accessibility guidelines. Beyond compliance, leveling the playing field for learning means instructional design that teaches effectively no matter what method a student uses to perceive it, whether via a screen reader or with closed captioning, whether using special fonts on a large monitor or using Braille.

To create effective learning for a diversity of students, *Into Literature* was designed using **Universal Design for Learning (UDL)** principles. UDL is a science-based framework developed by the Center for Applied Special Technology (CAST), a non-profit organization. UDL offers guidance for "improv[ing] and optimiz[ing] teaching and learning for all people based on scientific insights into how humans learn."

Into Literature was built with these principles in mind. As you review or use the program, ask yourself the questions in the chart. You'll discover that, through UDL and accessibility, *Into Literature* offers all students an equal opportunity to learn.

What is accessibility and why does it matter?

UNIVERSAL DESIGN FOR LEARNING FRAMEWORK

Provide Multiple Means of Engagement	Provide Multiple Means of Representation	Provide Multiple Means of Action and Expression
• Are there choices and autonomy for individual learners? • Is the content culturally relevant? • Does the learning experience foster collaboration and community? • Are there built-in opportunities for self-reflection? • Are assessments accompanied by meaningful feedback?	• Are there ways of customizing how the information is displayed? • Are there alternatives for both visual and auditory information? • Is vocabulary defined and explained? • Are concepts illustrated through multiple media, not just text? • Is background information supplied, when necessary?	• Are students encouraged to use multiple means of expression to demonstrate their knowledge? • Are digital experiences optimized for assistive technology? • Are there graphic organizers, note-taking devices, and checklists in place to help students manage and comprehend information?

Supporting All Learners

How does the *Into Literature* digital experience support all learners?

We Provide Accessible Formats

Into Literature is accessible. Students can use assistive technology, such as screen readers, to perceive and operate core digital materials. Large-type and Braille print publications for students are available through district request processes from the National Instructional Materials Access Center (NIMAC). Beyond the accessibility of core content for students, all users of assistive technology will find a friend in Ed, HMH's digital platform.

Here are some other digital capabilities of *Into Literature* to explore as you consider the diversity of learners in your classroom.

Feature	Benefits
Audio Support	All texts in the eBook include read-aloud audio, with human readers modeling fluency and expression. While some students may use this audio as an accommodation, this feature can help everyone strengthen reading comprehension. The **Read-Along Highlight** feature supports students in tracking their place more easily.
Display and Magnification Support	Most student components within *Into Literature* have dynamic layouts that respond to different device sizes in both landscape and portrait orientations. Not only will all students be able to read comfortably across devices, but students who rely on magnification and zooming will find the support they need. Encourage students to use the zoom function native to their browsers to magnify the content according to their reading needs or preferences.
Annotation and Note-Taking Tools	All student eBooks come with colorful highlighters, an underlining feature, bookmarks, and a self-organizing notebook. Marking up text while reading can help students comprehend story events and main ideas, track unfamiliar words, record evidence, and remember key details for writing and discussion.
Closed Captioning for Videos	**Peer Coach**, **Stream to Start**, and **Media Texts** have closed captioned videos. Closed captioning not only supports hearing-impaired students, but also supports those who prefer reading to listening, as well as anyone teaching or learning in a lively classroom where it might be hard to hear.

Bradbury creates an eerie mood.

View in Panel   Edit Note

Tips & Tricks!

Model close reading using the **annotations tools**. For example, you might have students choose one color for unfamiliar words and one color for author's craft. Invite them to jot down their questions and reactions to the text in their notes.

What accessibility options are available with *Into Literature* assessments?

Understand the Options

The **Diagnostic**, **Selection**, **Unit**, **Book Tests**, and **Guided Skills Practice** banks that come with *Into Literature* are not time-based, as timed assessments can be challenging for many learners who require accommodations. If you plan to use the digital tests on the platform to assess your students, take the time to acquaint them with the various accessibility options. If you decide to use the platform to create your own assessments, keep these suggestions in mind.

When students are taking an assessment, they can . . .

● use the **Accessibility Options** menu to change the color contrast and the font size, as well as exploring the options for zooming in and out on each item.

● use the **Response Masking** feature to help them narrow their choices and eliminate visual distraction.

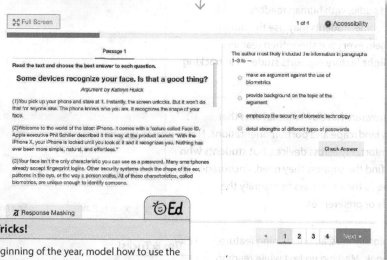

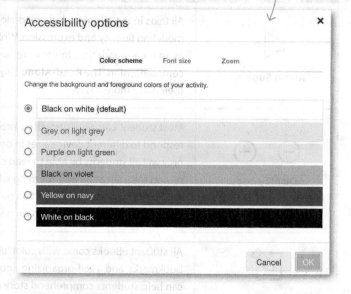

Tips & Tricks!

At the beginning of the year, model how to use the accessibility features in Ed before assigning any digital assessments. In particular, demonstrate how to use the **Response Masking** feature to help with answering questions.

When creating your own digital assessments, you can . . .

● consider reducing the number of distractors to make the choices more manageable for students.

● make sure that distractors are all distinct from one another and that there is one clear correct answer.

● model each digital item type as a whole class to make sure that the mechanics of answering the item are not a barrier to demonstrating understanding of the learning objective.

● write directions that are simple and clear. There should be no confusion about the task students are required to complete.

● think about whether you can assess the same learning objectives in different ways, such as with a performance assessment, rather than with a multiple-choice test. Remember—it's about demonstrating mastery of the concept, not the format of the test.

Designing Accessible Instruction

What tips should I keep in mind when designing accessible instruction?

Learn How They Learn

Your insight into how your students learn will help guide your decisions for using, repurposing, and supplementing the resources within *Into Literature*. You know what your students need better than we do! Use your own style to create instruction, keeping their diversity in mind. Here are some tips that might help.

- **Design instruction that incorporates more than one method of learning.** *Multiple means* is one of the foundational principles of UDL. If you teach aloud, also sketch or project pictures. If you teach with visuals, also provide reading.

- **Consider layout and presentation.** Font choices that work best for students with dyslexia (like Antique Olive), color choices that work best for students with color blindness (high contrast), and whitespace choices that work well for the visually impaired (generous) also work for students who need no accommodations. So why not start with these choices? Also consider presentation. Will you display the lesson on a whiteboard? If so, make sure the marker is thick enough to read from the back of the classroom.

- **Pair images and descriptions.** If you include images in any handouts or slides you develop, provide a description of those images to help visually impaired students understand their meaning.

- **Create captions.** Make sure any instructional videos you produce have captions. Sometimes audio descriptions or more descriptive transcripts are required.

- **Get descriptive.** If you post links or assignments to Ed or to a learning-management system, make sure they have meaningful titles that will make sense to students using screen readers or other assistive technology.

- **Check yourself.** Many popular tools, such as those created by Microsoft and Google®, are inherently accessible and have accessibility-checker features built into the software. Use them!

- **Think through alternatives.** Ask yourself: Will my students require an alternate means of demonstrating knowledge or completing the assignment? Adapt as necessary.

Remember that all of us have abilities—and limits to those abilities. Some limitations are permanent, and others are temporary. Thinking about people with permanent disabilities will result in instruction that benefits people universally.

Professional Learning

Surviving Your First Year in the Classroom

Getting Started

What should I do before students arrive?

Gather Resources

Take time to learn what resources are available to you. You may have more than what is apparent when you walk in your room.

- Take stock of the Student Edition. *Into Literature* is designed for students to have their own consumable print edition and/or digital edition each year. Is that the case at your school? If not, find out how other teachers manage.

- Familiarize yourself with the Teacher's Edition. Far from simply providing answers, this robust tool will help you plan and customize units and lessons; differentiate your teaching to accommodate students who struggle, advanced learners, and English learners; and pull in other resources.

- Make sure you have the credentials for Ed: Your Friend in Learning, the HMH digital platform. Think about how your students will access the platform. The Information Technology team in your school or district can get your students rostered.

- Check out the **Teacher's Corner** on Ed. It includes videos and tutorials that will help you get started with *Into Literature*, improve your craft, and address common teaching challenges.

- Talk to the school librarian and your department head about what novels and research materials are available, and how you can gain access to them.

- Remember that other teachers are your greatest resource. Don't be afraid to ask the veterans in your school for help.

Make Some Plans and Organize Your Room

Figure out which elements of the curriculum are set by your administration and which are up to you. Even if you are working from a mandated list of texts and skills, you will want to have some activities on hand that can keep your students engaged while reinforcing concepts. Ask veteran teachers where they look for ideas.

Make the classroom yours. You don't have to go overboard and fill every space. You'll want room to show students' work as they complete it, and to display anchor charts and reminders that you work on together. But you can add visual interest by showcasing the covers from popular novels, promote positive values by including literary or motivational quotations, and help students get to know you by representing your own interests.

Getting Started

What should I do my first week?

Tips & Tricks!

Follow up the essay with an interest inventory. Write a variety of genres on a flip chart or on pieces of paper taped around the room, and have students write their name next to genres they like.

Get to Know Your Class

Get to know your students through a combination of fun games, an introduction to academics, and assessment.

- Play **a game of blobs and lines**, where students organize themselves in groups or lines according to prompts you call out. You can use variations on this game throughout the year to get students moving and have them take a position on topics introduced in class.

- Read **"An Absolutely, Positively Must-Read Essay About Reading"** on page FM24 and use it as a jumping-off point for a discussion about what students like to read.

- Administer the **HMH Growth Measure**, an adaptive student assessment that measures reading skills and progress, so that you know where your students are starting from and can monitor their growth over the course of the year.

Blobs and Lines Prompts

Tell students to organize themselves

- in an alphabetical line by first name
- in an alphabetical line by last name
- into groups according to who prefers graphic novels and who prefers prose
- into groups according to who prefers science fiction and who prefers realistic fiction

Establish Routines and Set Expectations

You may feel nervous your first few weeks in the classroom, but it's important to project authority and confidence. Fake it until you make it, and know that you won't be the first new teacher to use this trusted strategy.

- Introduce key expectations and routines to your class. Will you have students do a Bell Ringer activity each day? Complete a **Response Log** about the unit's Essential Question at the end of each selection? Tell students what you expect from them, and what they can expect from you.

- Explain grading and preview major milestones. If there's a big project or a well-known unit that students will be working toward, create excitement around it.

- Begin the first unit. Use the **Spark Your Learning** activities in the Student Edition to continue to get to know your students and help them to know each other.

- Assign the first selection. Choose something high-interest that is likely to appeal to a large number of students.

How should I organize my students?

Choose a Purposeful Seating Plan

Whether students are grouped at tables or seated at individual desks, a seating map is a powerful tool. Revise it throughout the year in response to your students' behavior, growth, and academic and social needs.

- Group struggling readers with advanced readers. Encourage higher performers to offer assistance and feedback to students who are having more of a struggle.

- Establish routines for how individuals or groups should move around the room or function independently. Discuss expectations first and model the behavior you wish to see.

- Seat students with behavioral needs closest to wherever you are the most stationary. Proximity is a great way to redirect misbehavior without disrupting the lesson or drawing attention to the student.

- Create a clear and wide path by which you can circulate the room with ease. If you know you spend time conferring with specific students, seat them in areas where your back won't be turned to the rest of the class when you talk to them.

What activities can I use for grouping or independent learning?

Use Flexible Grouping Strategies

Students shouldn't only work in groups with those they're seated with. Variety will help keep them engaged. The **Lesson Planning Guides** and notes in the Teacher's Edition suggest activities designed for whole-class, independent, and small-group learning, including partner activities. Try different strategies for creating groups.

- Group students who struggle with the same skill so that they can receive remediation together.

- Ask students to count off by six and move to work with others who have the same number they do for that day.

- Have students group themselves by birthdays. Those born in January and February work together, those born in March and April work together, and so on.

👥 Small Group

Think-Pair-Share

- After students have read and analyzed "Dark They Were, And Golden-Eyed," ask: What mysteries are left unexplained at the end of the story? How does the story's theme apply to real life?

- Have students think about the questions individually and take notes.

- Have pairs discuss their ideas about the question.

- Ask pairs to share their responses with the class.

Managing Your Class

Set Expectations, Model, and Reflect

Dealing with behavior and classroom management might be a challenge at first, but you've got this. Allow yourself to dial back the amount of material you cover as you figure out management strategies that work in your classroom.

- Make sure you're familiar with any school-wide expectations or behavior programs. Reinforce these with the messaging in your class.

- Keep an eye on students. Face them as much as possible. If a student is being disruptive, try focusing attention on that person with a glance, or by asking a question about the lesson. Often you'll be able to redirect behavior without calling that student out.

- Get students involved. Create classroom jobs that rotate each week or month, and invite students to discuss and contribute to classroom rules. Students who feel that it's "their" classroom will work harder to make it a positive environment.

How can I promote positive student behavior?

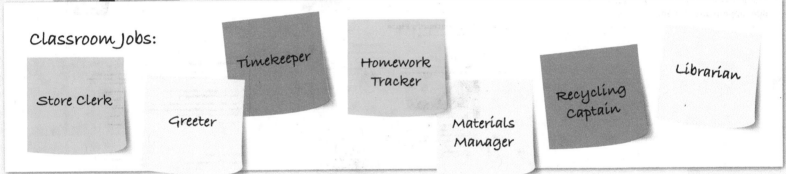

Classroom Jobs:

Store Clerk

Greeter

Timekeeper

Homework Tracker

Materials Manager

Recycling Captain

Librarian

- Before group work, announce that you will call names at random to share out the group's take-aways. Each student in the group will earn a grade based on that one student's response. This ensures all students are invested in the discussion.

- Be mindful that research has shown we all carry unconscious biases, including racial bias. Question your own assumptions and behavior, and reflect on whether you treat different students differently for the same misbehavior. Be ready to adjust your teaching practice as you learn more about your students and yourself.

How can I instill a love of reading?

Tips & Tricks!

The **Text Library** offers selections in a wide range of genres and Lexile® levels. Find opportunities to let students explore the offerings in the Lexile® ranges appropriate to them.

Offer Variety and Choice

Give students opportunities to connect their reading material with their lives.

- Offer reading material that students can see themselves in. Care has been taken so that the texts in *Into Literature* represent the diversity of the world, but you'll want to go beyond that. The website *We Need Diverse Books* is a resource that can help you find titles and authors that appeal to a wide range of cultures and identities.

- Surround students with good books. Work with your school or community librarian as you build your own classroom library. Refer to organizations such as the YALAB (a division of the American Library Association) to keep abreast of new, popular, and award-winning books for young adults.

- Encourage students to make personal connections to what they read, including connections to movies and pop culture. The **Engage Your Brain** activities that open each lesson often offer opportunities to do this.

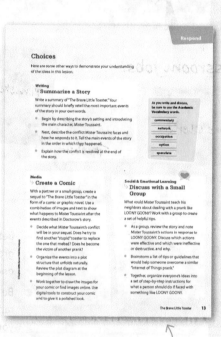

- Allow students to respond to their reading in a variety of ways. Not everything has to be assessed with a quiz or an academic writing assignment. The **Choices** activities at the end of each lesson offer chances for students to respond creatively to assigned reading. For independent reading, you can have students show their understanding through a conversation with you, a video summary, or a poster that shows key literary elements.

- Model your own reading life. If you communicate with students by email, include the title of the book you're reading as part of your signature. Read chunks of text aloud to demonstrate how stories can come alive.

Avoiding Burnout

How do I spend less time grading?

Tips & Tricks!

Choose student work from another class period to provide models.

Don't Try to Do It All

Grading, especially the grading of writing, can be an English language arts teacher's biggest time commitment. But there are ways to make it more manageable.

- You do not have to personally grade every assignment. Consider informally monitoring students' progress on lower-stakes assignments.

- **Ed** If you administer **Selection** and **Unit Tests** online, the platform will do the majority of the work for you. You do need to grade open-response items, but you have the ability to remove them from the test before assigning it.

- During writing time, circulate around the room, pausing to offer explicit feedback to students you know are struggling. This will save you time later.

- Use the **Revision Guide** that accompanies each writing task to model how to evaluate an example of student writing. Then allow students to use the same guide to evaluate each other's drafts.

- **Ed** Use **Writable** tools. Functions like **Turn It In, Revision Aid**, and anonymous peer reviews can end up saving you time. See "Building Better Writers" in this guide for more details.

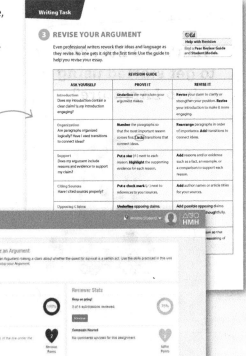

Keep Calm and Carry On

The first year in the classroom can definitely be challenging. You have to familiarize yourself with the material, prepare for every lesson, and learn how to meet the requirements of your administration. And that's before the students walk into the classroom! At times, you may feel like you're not getting through to the young learners seated before you. But, more often than not, you probably are, even if they don't show it right away. And if things don't go well today, there's always tomorrow, or next week.

Remember that teaching is a practice that you will refine over time. You don't have to do everything perfectly. It's okay to make mistakes. Seek out the company of other teachers. Learn from them, laugh with them, and take all the help that they'll give you. Soon you'll be in a position to help guide someone else on how to survive and thrive in this meaningful and interesting career.

What if I'm not good at this?

Growing Your Craft with HMH Literacy Solutions™

Engaging in Professional Learning

What's the best way to get started using *Into Literature*?

Take the Getting Started Training

Service Training is an important part of using *Into Literature*, and it's designed to be on-going and flexible enough to meet your needs without overwhelming you. The **Getting Started** professional learning session is your first step. It's focused on preparing you for the first few weeks of school.

● Watch classroom videos to see master teachers in action.

● Read articles and get tips from fellow *Into Literature* teachers and other program experts.

● Connect with HMH coaches and thought leaders via live events.

How can I make sure I'm getting the most out of *Into Literature*?

Follow up with HMH Literacy Solutions™

As you use the program, questions will arise. **HMH Literacy Solutions™** provides Follow-Up opportunities throughout the year. These shorter sessions allow you to stay engaged and build your expertise in a manageable way. Your school or district can choose from a variety of follow-up topics, including:

● Maximize Learning with Online Resources

● Plan Instruction to Meet Students' Needs

● Make Literacy Accessible for All with Differentiation

● Support English Learners in Reading, Writing, Speaking, and Listening

● Deepen Text Analysis with Notice & Note Close Reading Strategies

● Cultivate Student Voice and Ownership through the Writing Process

● Use **Writable** to Strengthen Writing through Practice, Feedback, and Revision

Writable

Getting Started Checklist

☑ Visit and bookmark Ed

☑ Take the Getting Started training

☑ Determine the technology needs for your classroom and consider the following questions:

• Will your students primarily use the print or online version of the Student Edition? Will they use different versions for whole-class instruction and small collaborative groups?

• When and how will students access the digital Reading, Writing, Grammar, Vocabulary, and Speaking and Listening Resources?

• Will students access eBooks during independent reading?

☑ As you plan your first unit of instruction, consider teaching one selection according to our recommendations, to get to know all the available resources and features.

Tips & Tricks!

Visit **Teacher's Corner** on Ed and select **Program Support** to dig deeper into specific areas of *Into Literature*. You will find videos, articles, classroom videos, and more.

Participating in Blended Coaching

How can I grow as a teacher and improve student outcomes?

Get Some Coaching

HMH Literacy Solutions™ offers personalized instructional coaching services in districts that have chosen to participate. Coaches use the **Literacy Solutions Instructional Practices Inventory** to focus on both *Into Literature* implementation and evidence-based instructional practices and strategies that increase student outcomes.

To make it easy for you and your HMH coach to stay connected, share resources, upload and reflect on classroom videos, and make continuing progress on learning goals, you will have access to the **HMH Coaching Studio** platform.

HMH Into Literature Blended Coaching Services provide:

- model lessons that illustrate instructional techniques
- support for implementing effective teaching practices
- differentiation strategies to meet the needs of all students
- focus on developing and deepening content knowledge
- analysis of student work samples to assess learning and determine instructional next steps
- facilitation of professional learning communities, cadres, and collaborative learning

Growing Your Craft with Teacher's Corner

Getting Started

What is Teacher's Corner?

A One-Click Solution for Professional Learning

We know that for some things, just-in-time help can be more effective than periodic in-person trainings. **Teacher's Corner** is a section on the learning platform Ed where you can get tips for using *Into Literature*, help with lesson planning, and ideas for improving your instructional practice exactly when you need them. With Teacher's Corner, you have access to on-demand professional learning and teaching support via Ed anytime, anywhere.

- Watch classroom videos to see master teachers in action.

- Read articles and get tips from fellow *Into Literature* teachers and other program experts.

- Connect with HMH coaches and thought leaders via live events.

Explore Recommendations Based on What You Need Now

Choose from a library of bite-size, curated professional learning resources that were designed to be immediately applicable. Some of these can be read or viewed in the time it takes to drink a cup of coffee. Others are longer, but still short enough to fit into your day. The resources come in a variety of media types and are organized into four areas.

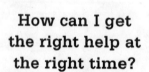

How can I get the right help at the right time?

- **Getting Started** offers introductions to *Into Literature* and help with back-to-school planning.

- **Program Support** helps you troubleshoot and get the most out of *Into Literature* as you deepen your teaching.

- **Teacher's Breakroom** gives information about general best practices and lesson ideas, and provides inspiration for teachers across grades and disciplines.

- **Live Events** allows you to register for sessions that are relevant to your needs.

5 Tips for Pacing and Prioritizing Instruction with Into Literature

I once heard someone say: "The minute someone develops a pacing guide, it's out of date." Every school has different state and district mandated instructional days, literacy block/ELA minutes, structures, student numbers, and student needs. The art of teaching is how to use the resources to meet the needs of our students! As a special educator, intervention teacher, ELA and Reading Coordinator, I loved working with teams of teachers to dig into that puzzle. I hope my tips and tricks for pacing and prioritizing will help in your quest to pace and prioritize instruction in your *Into Literature* classroom! Remember: it's a journey, not an event!

Tip 1: Identify What Drives Your Instruction

When meeting with Into Literature teachers I often ask them a few guiding questions to help inform how to best support them with pacing and prioritizing instruction. As you begin your planning, consider the following:

- What are the student outcomes that you want to see?

- Which activities will be better suited to whole-group, small-group, or independent learning?

- Which activities will be appropriate for which students?

Learning from Peers and Experts

How can I learn from the teachers and coaches who are already using *Into Literature*?

Watch Teachers in Action

Many teachers told HMH that the most useful resources we could provide would be videos showing other teachers successfully using *Into Literature* in their classrooms. This growing bank of videos is available as part of a library of resources that provide authentic models and practical strategies addressing common questions.

How do people manage Response Logs?

How can I integrate writing into a unit?

How can I help my students use their prior knowledge?

How do I get my students started using Notice & Note?

What help is there for getting students to read closely?

Coach's Playbook

Into Literature

Setting Up Your Classroom with *Into Literature*

Best practices for planning a productive school year.

⏱ 10 minutes | Video

How can I connect with other teachers and program experts?

Register for Live Events

Whether you have a question, need implementation advice, or want to keep up with the latest thinking on educational trends, **Live Events** offers you opportunities to connect with HMH coaches and each other. You can register for online sessions that feature everything from groundbreaking new author research to group discussions facilitated by other teachers.

Into Literature Unit Planning Guides

Get acquainted with each middle-school grade level of *HMH Into Literature* by previewing the instructional design of each unit. As you review each **Unit Planning Guide** in Grades 6–8, notice

- the unit topic and essential question
- the texts and authors included in the unit, including details about genre, pacing, and Lexile®
- the key skills in reading, writing, vocabulary, and language
- the independent reading options for the unit in the **Reader's Choice** section
- the cumulative tasks in writing and speaking and listening
- digital resources that can support you in teaching each text

Discovering Your Voice

Analyze & Apply

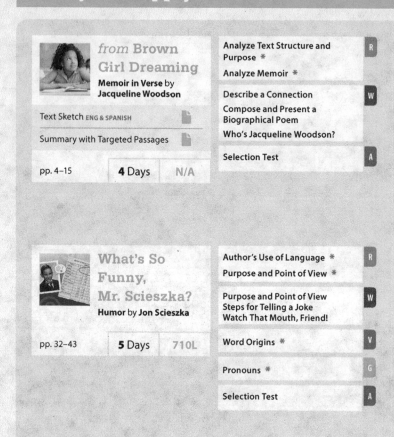

from **Brown Girl Dreaming**

Memoir in Verse by **Jacqueline Woodson**

Text Sketch ENG & SPANISH

Summary with Targeted Passages

pp. 4–15 | **4** Days | N/A

Analyze Text Structure and Purpose *
Analyze Memoir * **R**

Describe a Connection
Compose and Present a Biographical Poem
Who's Jacqueline Woodson? **W**

Selection Test **A**

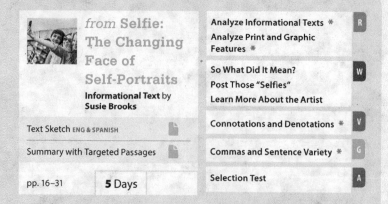

from **Selfie: The Changing Face of Self-Portraits**

Informational Text by **Susie Brooks**

Text Sketch ENG & SPANISH

Summary with Targeted Passages

pp. 16–31 | **5** Days

Analyze Informational Texts *
Analyze Print and Graphic Features * **R**

So What Did It Mean?
Post Those "Selfies"
Learn More About the Artist **W**

Connotations and Denotations * **V**

Commas and Sentence Variety * **G**

Selection Test **A**

What's So Funny, Mr. Scieszka?

Humor by **Jon Scieszka**

pp. 32–43 | **5** Days | 710L

Author's Use of Language *
Purpose and Point of View * **R**

Purpose and Point of View
Steps for Telling a Joke
Watch That Mouth, Friend! **W**

Word Origins * **V**

Pronouns * **G**

Selection Test **A**

Collaborate & Compare

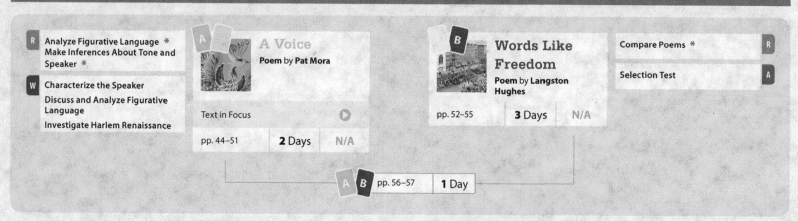

R Analyze Figurative Language *
Make Inferences About Tone and Speaker *

W Characterize the Speaker
Discuss and Analyze Figurative Language
Investigate Harlem Renaissance

A **A Voice**

Poem by **Pat Mora**

Text in Focus ▶

pp. 44–51 | **2** Days | N/A

B **Words Like Freedom**

Poem by **Langston Hughes**

pp. 52–55 | **3** Days | N/A

Compare Poems * **R**

Selection Test **A**

A **B** pp. 56–57 | **1** Day

SKILLS

R	Reading
W	Writing/Speaking & Listening/Media
V	Vocabulary

RESOURCES

G	Grammar
A	Assessment

* Skills covered on Unit Assessment

- ▶ Video
- 📄 Document

Collaborate & Compare

R Trace and Evaluate an Argument *
Determine an Author's Purpose *

W Compose an Argument
Create and Present "The Perfect Selfie"
Put that Phone Away, Please!

V Context Clues *

G Spell Commonly Confused Words Correctly *

A

Better Than Words: Say It with a Selfie
Argument by **Gloria Chang**

pp. 58–67	**2** Days	1050L

B

MENTOR TEXT

OMG, Not *Another* Selfie!
Argument by **Shermakaye Bass**

Close Read Screencast	▶
Text Sketch ENG & SPANISH	📄
Summary with Targeted Passages	📄

pp. 68–77	**3** Days	1070L

R Compare and Evaluate Augments *

A Selection Test

A **B** | pp. 78–79 | **1** Day |

Reader's Choice

Find summaries and activities related to Reader's Choice texts on pp. 80–81, and find Reader's Choice texts and tests online.

I Was a Skinny Tomboy Kid
Poem by
Alma Luz Villanueva
N/A

Words are Birds
Poem by **Francisco X. Alarcón**
N/A

Eleven
Short Story by **Sandra Cisneros**
990L

On Dragonwings
Short Story by **Lucy D. Ford**
620

Carved on the Walls
Informational Text by **Judy Yung**
1060L

Unit Tasks

Discovering Your Voice

pp. 82–91	**5** Days

W Write an Argument

G Use Pronouns

W Reflect & Extend
- Write a Memoir
- Create a Photo Collage

A Discovering Your Voice Unit Test

Never Give Up

Analyze & Apply

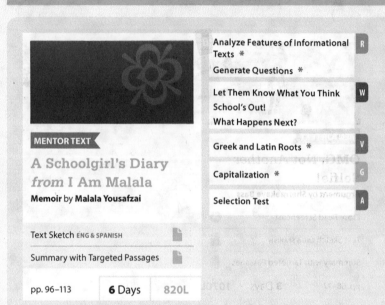

MENTOR TEXT

A Schoolgirl's Diary
from I Am Malala

Memoir by Malala Yousafzai

Text Sketch ENG & SPANISH 📄

Summary with Targeted Passages 📄

| pp. 96–113 | **6** Days | 820L |

Analyze Features of Informational Texts * — R
Generate Questions *

Let Them Know What You Think — W
School's Out!
What Happens Next?

Greek and Latin Roots * — V

Capitalization * — G

Selection Test — A

Speech to the Young: Speech to the Progress-Toward

Poem by Gwendolyn Brooks

| pp. 114–121 | **4** Days | N/A |

Analyze Poetic Forms * — R
Make Inferences About Theme *

A "Speech" for Someone Who Needs It — W
Video Interpretation
"You Will Be Right"

Selection Test — A

Collaborate & Compare

Analyze Plot and Character * — R
Analyze Setting *

There's Something About John — W
Compare and Contrast Experiences
How Have Schools Changed?

Thesaurus * — V

Sentence Patterns * — G

A

The First Day of School

Short Story by R.V. Cassill

Text in Focus ▶

Close Read Screencast ▶

| pp. 122–137 | **5** Days | 790L |

B

New Kid

Graphic Novel by Jerry Craft

| pp. 138–157 | **4** Days | N/A |

Analyze Plot and Character * — R
Analyze Setting and Theme *
Compare Time Periods *

Analyze the Characters — W
Roundtable
A Vlog for the New Kids

Selection Test — A

A B | pp. 158–159 | **1** Day

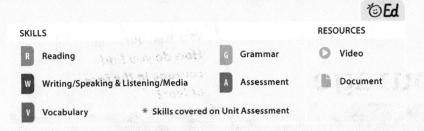

SKILLS

R Reading

W Writing/Speaking & Listening/Media

V Vocabulary

RESOURCES

G Grammar

A Assessment

▶ Video

📄 Document

* Skills covered on Unit Assessment

Reader's Choice

Find summaries and activities related to Reader's Choice texts on pp. 160–161 and find Reader's Choice texts and tests online.

Paul Revere's Ride
Poem by **Henry Wadsworth Longfellow**

N/A

Damon and Pythias
Dramatized by **Fan Kissen**

N/A

The Road Not Taken
Poem by **Robert Frost**

N/A

Education First *from* Malala's Speech to the United Nations
Speech by **Malala Yousafzai**

870L

Unit Tasks

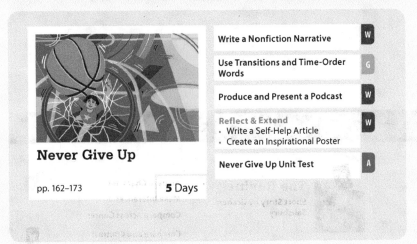

Never Give Up

pp. 162–173

5 Days

Write a Nonfiction Narrative **W**

Use Transitions and Time-Order Words **G**

Produce and Present a Podcast **W**

Reflect & Extend **W**
• Write a Self-Help Article
• Create an Inspirational Poster

Never Give Up Unit Test **A**

Finding Courage

ESSENTIAL QUESTION:
? *How do you find courage in the face of fear?*

Analyze & Apply

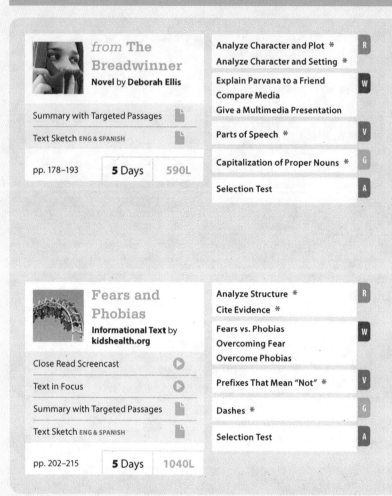

from **The Breadwinner**
Novel by **Deborah Ellis**

Summary with Targeted Passages

Text Sketch ENG & SPANISH

pp. 178–193 | **5 Days** | 590L

Analyze Character and Plot * | **R**
Analyze Character and Setting *

Explain Parvana to a Friend | **W**
Compare Media
Give a Multimedia Presentation

Parts of Speech * | **V**

Capitalization of Proper Nouns * | **G**

Selection Test | **A**

Fears and Phobias
Informational Text by **kidshealth.org**

Close Read Screencast ▶
Text in Focus ▶
Summary with Targeted Passages
Text Sketch ENG & SPANISH

pp. 202–215 | **5 Days** | 1040L

Analyze Structure * | **R**
Cite Evidence *

Fears vs. Phobias | **W**
Overcoming Fear
Overcome Phobias

Prefixes That Mean "Not" * | **V**

Dashes * | **G**

Selection Test | **A**

Life Doesn't Frighten Me
Poem by **Maya Angelou**

pp. 194–201 | **3 Days** | N/A

Explain Speaker * | **R**
Analyze Structure: Repetition and Refrain *

Compose a Lyric Poem | **W**
Present a Poem
Compare and Contrast Versions of a Poem

Selection Test | **A**

▶ **Wired for Fear**
Video by the **California Science Center**

pp. 216–219 | **2 Days** | Media

Analyze Media * | **W**
Integrate Information
Produce a Podcast
Discover the Power of Fear

Selection Test | **A**

Collaborate & Compare

R Analyze Structure
Determine Meanings *

W Report on Research
Driven by Fear
Advertise a Service

V Synonyms and Antonyms *

G Commas *

A **Embarrassed? Blame Your Brain**
Informational Text by **Jennifer Connor-Smith**

pp. 220–233 | **4 Days** | 960L

B **The Ravine**
Short Story by **Graham Salisbury**

Close Read Screencast ▶
Text in Focus ▶

pp. 234–251 | **5 Days** | 640L

Analyze Character | **R**
Make Inferences *
Compare Across Genres *

Compare and Contrast | **W**
Coward or Hero?
Investigate Hawaiian Sports

Context Clues * | **V**

Varying Sentence Patterns * | **G**

Selection Test | **A**

A **B** | pp. 252–253 | **1 Day**

© Houghton Mifflin Harcourt Publishing Company • Image Credits: (tt) ©Ragne Kabanova/Shutterstock; (tr) ©Mihai Blanaru/Shutterstock; (cl) ©Bert123/Shutterstock; (cd) Wired for Fear: ©Created by Vogt Productions for the California Science Center Foundation; (bl) ©Tom Grill/Corbis/Getty Images; (br) ©MNStudio/Shutterstock

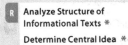
SKILLS

R	Reading
W	Writing/Speaking & Listening/Media
V	Vocabulary

RESOURCES

| G | Grammar |
| A | Assessment |

| ▶ | Video |
| 📄 | Document |

* Skills covered on Unit Assessment

Collaborate & Compare

R Analyze Structure of Informational Texts *
Determine Central Idea *

W Write a Summary
Investigate Advances in Flight
Discuss with a Small Group

V Multiple-Meaning Words *

G Adverbs and Adverb Clauses *

A

from Into the Air
Graphic Biography by Robert Burleigh

pp. 254–271 | **4** Days | 760L

B

MENTOR TEXT

from The Wright Brothers: How They Invented the Airplane
Biography by Russell Freedman

Text in Focus	▶
Summary with Targeted Passages	📄
Text Sketch ENG & SPANISH	📄

pp. 272–285 | **5** Days | 1100L

R Analyze Structure of Informational Texts *
Determine Key Ideas *
Compare Presentation of Events *

W What Happened?
Find the Main Idea
Never Give Up

V Resources *

G Transitions and Commas *

A Selection Test

A **B** pp. 286-287 | **1** Day

Reader's Choice

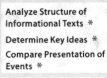

Find summaries and activities related to Reader's Choice texts on pp. 288–289 and find Reader's Choice texts and tests online.

Horrors
Poem by Lewis Carroll

N/A

Vanquishing the Hungry Chinese Zombie
Short Story by Claudine Gueh

760L

Running into Danger on an Alaskan Trail
Narrative Nonfiction by Cinthia Ritchie

860L

Face Your Fears: Choking Under Pressure Is Every Athlete's Worst Nightmare
Informational Text by Dana Hudepohl

870L

Unit Tasks

Finding Courage

pp. 290–301 | **5** Days

W Write an Informational Essay

G Compound and Complex Sentences

W Give a Presentation

W Reflect & Extend
• Write a Short Story
• Create a Vlog

A Finding Courage Unit Test

Through an Animal's Eyes

Analyze & Apply

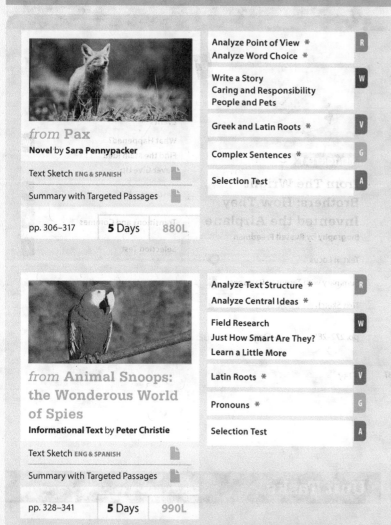

from **Pax**
Novel by **Sara Pennypacker**

Text Sketch ENG & SPANISH

Summary with Targeted Passages

pp. 306–317 | **5 Days** | 880L

Analyze Point of View *
Analyze Word Choice * **R**

Write a Story
Caring and Responsibility
People and Pets **W**

Greek and Latin Roots * **V**

Complex Sentences * **G**

Selection Test **A**

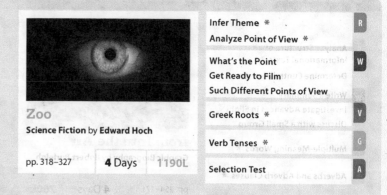

Zoo
Science Fiction by **Edward Hoch**

pp. 318–327 | **4 Days** | 1190L

Infer Theme *
Analyze Point of View * **R**

What's the Point
Get Ready to Film
Such Different Points of View **W**

Greek Roots * **V**

Verb Tenses * **G**

Selection Test **A**

from **Animal Snoops: the Wonderous World of Spies**
Informational Text by **Peter Christie**

Text Sketch ENG & SPANISH

Summary with Targeted Passages

pp. 328–341 | **5 Days** | 990L

Analyze Text Structure *
Analyze Central Ideas * **R**

Field Research
Just How Smart Are They?
Learn a Little More **W**

Latin Roots * **V**

Pronouns * **G**

Selection Test **A**

Collaborate & Compare

R Analyze Personification and
Imagery *
Paraphrase *

W Views of Wildlife
What Did You See? Here? Feel?
Discover the Truth About Wolves

 **A**

Animal Wisdom
Poem by **Nancy Wood**

pp. 342–348 | **2 Days** | N/A

 **B**

The Last Wolf
Poem by **Mary TallMountain**

pp. 349–353 | **3 Days** | N/A

Compare Themes * **R**

Selection Test **A**

A **B** pp. 354–355 | **1 Day**

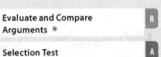

SKILLS

R Reading

W Writing/Speaking & Listening/Media

V Vocabulary   ***** Skills covered on Unit Assessment

RESOURCES

G Grammar

A Assessment

▷ Video

▢ Document

Collaborate & Compare

R Analyze Arguments *****

    Evaluate Arguments *****

W Take a Stand

    Create a PSA

    Do You *Really* Want One?

V Word Origins *****

G The Correct Word *****

MENTOR TEXT

Wild Animals Aren't Pets

Argument by **USA Today**

Close Read Screencast	▷
Text in Focus	▷
Text Sketch ENG & SPANISH	▢
Summary with Targeted Passages	▢

pp. 356–362	**2** Days	1120L

MENTOR TEXT

Let People Own Exotic Animals

Argument by **Zuzana Kokol**

Close Read Screencast	▷
Text in Focus	▷
Text Sketch ENG & SPANISH	▢
Summary with Targeted Passages	▢

pp. 363–369	**3** Days	1150L

R Evaluate and Compare Arguments *****

A Selection Test

A **B**	pp. 370–371	**1** Day

Reader's Choice

Find summaries and activities related to Reader's Choice texts on pp. 372–373 and find Reader's Choice texts and tests online.

The Caterpillar
Poem by **Robert Graves**

N/A

Tribute to the Dog
Speech by **George Graham Vest**

990L

The Flying Cat
Poem by **Naomi Shihab Nye**

N/A

Views on Zoos
Arguments

1000L

The Pod
Short Story by **Maureen Crane Wartski**

830L

Unit Tasks

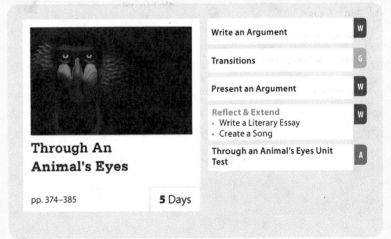

Through An Animal's Eyes

pp. 374–385	**5** Days

W Write an Argument

G Transitions

W Present an Argument

W Reflect & Extend
- Write a Literary Essay
- Create a Song

A Through an Animal's Eyes Unit Test

Surviving the Unthinkable

ESSENTIAL QUESTION:
What does it take to be a survivor?

Analyze & Apply

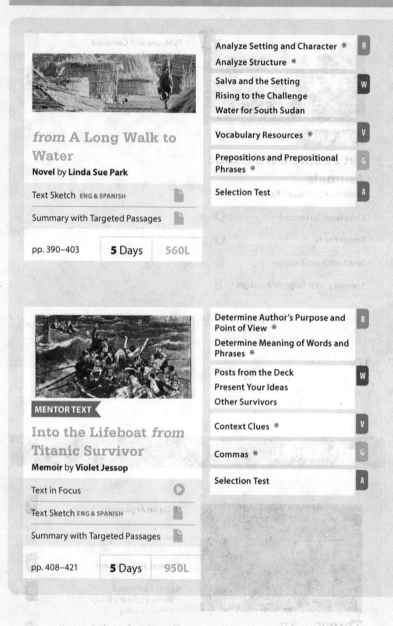

from A Long Walk to Water

Novel by **Linda Sue Park**

Text Sketch ENG & SPANISH

Summary with Targeted Passages

pp. 390–403 | **5 Days** | 560L

- Analyze Setting and Character * — R
- Analyze Structure *
- Salva and the Setting — W
- Rising to the Challenge
- Water for South Sudan
- Vocabulary Resources * — V
- Prepositions and Prepositional Phrases * — G
- Selection Test — A

ETHIOPIA

KENYA

▶ Salva's Story

Documentary by **POVRoseMedia**

pp. 404–407 | **2 Days** | Media

- Integrate Information from Media * — R
- Summary Timeline — W
- Compare and Contrast Presentation of Events
- The Lost Boys
- Selection Test — A

MENTOR TEXT

Into the Lifeboat from Titanic Survivor

Memoir by **Violet Jessop**

Text in Focus ▶

Text Sketch ENG & SPANISH

Summary with Targeted Passages

pp. 408–421 | **5 Days** | 950L

- Determine Author's Purpose and Point of View * — R
- Determine Meaning of Words and Phrases *
- Posts from the Deck — W
- Present Your Ideas
- Other Survivors
- Context Clues * — V
- Commas * — G
- Selection Test — A

😊Ed

SKILLS

RESOURCES

R Reading

W Writing/Speaking & Listening/Media

V Vocabulary

G Grammar

A Assessment

▶ Video

📄 Document

* Skills covered on Unit Assessment

Collaborate & Compare

R Analyze Free Verse *
Analyze Figurative Language *

W Write a Poem
What Went Right?
Responders

A

from After the Hurricane
Poem by **Rita Williams-Garcia**

Close Read Screencast ▶

pp. 422–435 | **5** Days | N/A

B

from Ninth Ward
Novel by
Jewell Parker Rhodes

pp. 436–447 | **5** Days | 570L

Analyze Setting * **R**
Analyze Language *
Compare Across Genres *

Texts from a Rooftop **W**
Create a Poster
Discover the Ninth Ward

Context Clues * **V**

Pronouns * **G**

Selection Test **A**

A **B** pp. 448–449 | **1** Day

😊Ed

Reader's Choice

Find summaries and activities related to Reader's Choice texts on pp. 450–451 and find Reader's Choice texts and tests online.

Watcher: After Katrina, 2005
Poem by **Natasha D. Trethewey** | N/A

The Day I Didn't Go to the Pool
Short Story by **Leslie J. Wyatt** | 790L

Tuesday of the Other June
Short Story by **Norma Fox Mazer** | 570L

In Event of Moon Disaster
Speech by **Bill Safire** | 900L

Ready: Preparing Your Pets for Emergencies Makes Sense
Informational Text by **Ready.gov** | 1070L

Unit Tasks

Surviving the Unthinkable

pp. 452–461 | **5** Days

Write an Explanatory Essay **W**

Consistency in Style and Tone **G**

Reflect & Extend **W**
· Create an Infographic
· Compare and Contrast Accounts

Surviving the Unthinkable
Unit Test **A**

Hidden Truths

ESSENTIAL QUESTION:
What hidden truths about people and the world are revealed in stories?

Analyze & Apply

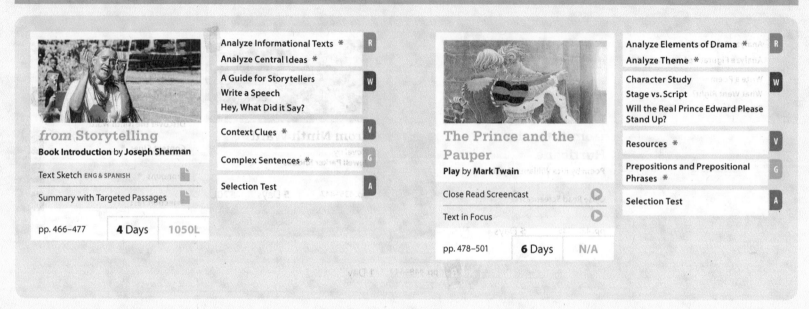

from Storytelling
Book Introduction by **Joseph Sherman**

Text Sketch ENG & SPANISH

Summary with Targeted Passages

| pp. 466–477 | **4** Days | 1050L |

Analyze Informational Texts * R
Analyze Central Ideas *

A Guide for Storytellers W
Write a Speech
Hey, What Did it Say?

Context Clues * V

Complex Sentences * G

Selection Test A

The Prince and the Pauper
Play by **Mark Twain**

Close Read Screencast ▶

Text in Focus ▶

| pp. 478–501 | **6** Days | N/A |

Analyze Elements of Drama * R
Analyze Theme *

Character Study W
Stage vs. Script
Will the Real Prince Edward Please Stand Up?

Resources * V

Prepositions and Prepositional Phrases * G

Selection Test A

Collaborate & Compare

R Analyze Poetic Forms *
Analyze Allusions *

W Paraphrase Those Difficult Lines *
Was the Story *Really* that Bad?
Mix and Match

Archetype
Poem by **Margarita Engle**

| pp. 502–509 | **2** Days | N/A |

Fairy-tale Logic
Poem by **A.E. Stallings**

| pp. 510–513 | **3** Days | N/A |

Compare Poems * R

Selection Test A

A B | pp. 514–515 | **1** Day |

SKILLS

R Reading

W Writing/Speaking & Listening/Media

V Vocabulary

RESOURCES

G Grammar

A Assessment

▶ Video

📄 Document

* Skills covered on Unit Assessment

ⓔEd

Collaborate & Compare

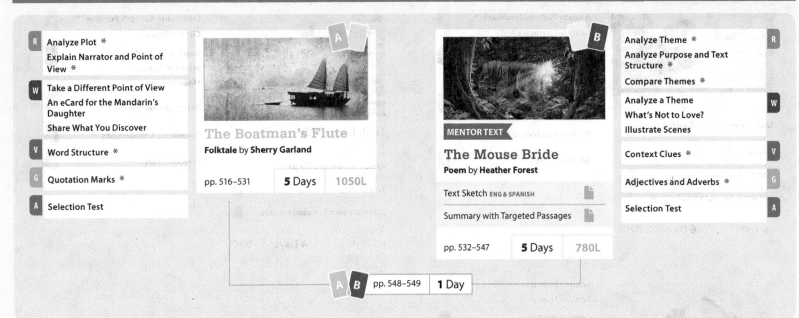

R Analyze Plot *
Explain Narrator and Point of View *

W Take a Different Point of View
An eCard for the Mandarin's Daughter
Share What You Discover

V Word Structure *

G Quotation Marks *

A Selection Test

The Boatman's Flute

Folktale by **Sherry Garland**

pp. 516–531   **5** Days   1050L

MENTOR TEXT

The Mouse Bride

Poem by **Heather Forest**

Text Sketch ENG & SPANISH 📄

Summary with Targeted Passages 📄

pp. 532–547   **5** Days   780L

R Analyze Theme *
Analyze Purpose and Text Structure *
Compare Themes *

W Analyze a Theme
What's Not to Love?
Illustrate Scenes

V Context Clues *

G Adjectives and Adverbs *

A Selection Test

A B   pp. 548–549   **1** Day

ⓔEd

Reader's Choice

Find summaries and activities related to Reader's Choice texts on pp. 550–551 and find Reader's Choice texts and tests online.

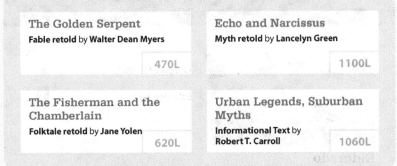

The Golden Serpent
Fable retold by **Walter Dean Myers**
470L

Echo and Narcissus
Myth retold by **Lancelyn Green**
1100L

The Fisherman and the Chamberlain
Folktale retold by **Jane Yolen**
620L

Urban Legends, Suburban Myths
Informational Text by **Robert T. Carroll**
1060L

Unit Tasks

Hidden Truths

pp. 552–561   **5** Days

W Write a Short Story

G Pay Attention to Style

W Reflect & Extend
• Write a Literary Analysis
• Create a Movie Trailer

A Hidden Truths Unit Test

Reality Check

ESSENTIAL QUESTION:
What can blur the lines between what's real and what's not?

Analyze & Apply

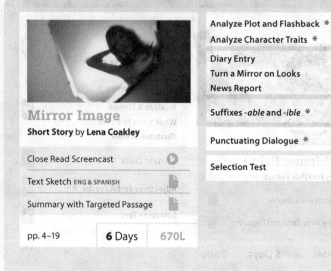

Mirror Image
Short Story by **Lena Coakley**

Close Read Screencast ▶

Text Sketch ENG & SPANISH

Summary with Targeted Passage

pp. 4–19 | **6** Days | 670L

Analyze Plot and Flashback * — **R**
Analyze Character Traits *

Diary Entry — **W**
Turn a Mirror on Looks
News Report

Suffixes -*able* and -*ible* * — **V**

Punctuating Dialogue * — **G**

Selection Test — **A**

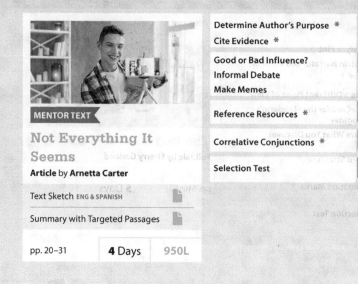

MENTOR TEXT

Not Everything It Seems
Article by **Arnetta Carter**

Text Sketch ENG & SPANISH

Summary with Targeted Passages

pp. 20–31 | **4** Days | 950L

Determine Author's Purpose * — **R**
Cite Evidence *

Good or Bad Influence? — **W**
Informal Debate
Make Memes

Reference Resources — **V**

Correlative Conjunctions * — **G**

Selection Test — **A**

Two Legs or One?
Folktale by **Joseph Sherman**

pp. 32–41 | **3** Days | 600L

Analyze Folktales — **R**
Analyze Humor

Critique the Twists — **W**
Trickster Tales
Retell the Tale

Glossary * — **V**

Commas * — **G**

Selection Test — **A**

Collaborate & Compare

R Analyze Rhyme *
Analyze Rhyme Scheme and
Mood *

W A Mystery Poem
Illustrate Sketchy Moments
Perform a Choral Reading

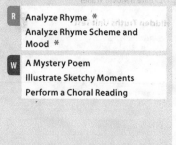

A

The Song of Wandering Aengus
Poem by **W.B. Yeats**

pp. 42–49 | **2** Days | N/A

B

Eldorado
Poem by **Edgar Allen Poe**

pp. 50–53 | **3** Days | N/A

Compare Moods * — **R**

Selection Test — **A**

A B | pp. 54–55 | **1** Day

SKILLS

R Reading

W Writing/Speaking & Listening/Media

V Vocabulary

RESOURCES

G Grammar

A Assessment

▶ Video

📄 Document

* Skills covered on Unit Assessment

Collaborate & Compare

R Analyze Narrator *
Analyze Graphic Novels *

W Write a Character Analysis
Create a Storyboard
Panel Discussion

V Word Origins *

G Complex Sentences:
Subordinating Conjunctions *

A

from Monster

Screenplay by **Walter Dean Myers**

pp. 56–68 | **3** Days | N/A

B

from Monster

Graphic Novel by **Walter Dean Myers**
adapted by **Guy A. Sims,** illustrated by
Dawud Anyabwile

pp. 69–81 | **2** Days | N/A

Compare Versions * **R**

Selection Test **A**

A B | pp. 82–83 | **1** Day

Reader's Choice

Find summaries and activities related to Reader's Choice texts on pp. 84–85, and find Reader's Choice texts and tests online.

Way Too Cool
Short Story by **Brenda Woods**
610L

He—y, Come on Ou—t
Short Story by **Shinichi Hoshi**
840L

Forever New
Informational Text by **Dan Risch**
1030L

A Priceless Lesson in Humility
Personal Essay by
Felipe Morales
930L

Unit Tasks

Reality Check

pp. 86–95 | **5** Days

Write an Informative Essay **W**

Capitalize Proper Adjectives **G**

Reflect & Extend **W**
- Create a Sketchnote
- Write a Short Story

Reality Check Unit Test **A**

Take Control

Analyze & Apply

Heartbeat
Short Story by **David Yoo**

Text Sketch ENG & SPANISH

Summary with Targeted Passages

pp. 100–111 | **5** Days | 820L

Analyze Character * [R]
Analyze Conflict *

Note of Apology [W]
Father-Son Role-Play
Self-Help Infographic

Greek Prefixes * [V]

Types of Clauses * [G]

Selection Test [A]

The Flight of Icarus
Myth retold by **Sally Benson**

Close Read Screencast ▶

Text in Focus ▶

pp. 112–123 | **4** Days | 1090L

Analyze Myth * [R]
Determine Themes *

Blog Post [W]
Supporting a Grieving Person
Virtual-Reality Proposal

Latin Suffixes * [V]

Commas and Coordinate [G]
Adjectives *

Selection Test [A]

Icarus's Flight
Poem by **Stephen Dobyns**

pp. 124–131 | **4** Days | N/A

Analyze Form in Poetry * [R]
Analyze Word Choice *

Poem [W]
Critique the Poem
Wing Diagram

Selection Test [A]

Rogue Wave
Short Story by **Theodore Taylor**

Close Read Screencast ▶

Text in Focus ▶

Text Sketch ENG & SPANISH

Summary with Targeted Passages

pp. 132–151 | **6** Days | 970L

Analyze Plot * [R]
Make Inferences *

Disaster Film Proposal [W]
Coping with Disasters
Rogue Waves

Latin Roots * [V]

Sentence Structure * [G]

Selection Test [A]

MENTOR TEXT

Women in Aviation
History Writing by **Patricia and Fredrick McKissack**

Text Sketch ENG & SPANISH

Summary with Targeted Passages

pp. 152–165 | **5** Days | 1120L

Determine Author's Purpose * [R]
Cite Evidence and Evaluate Details *

Tribute to Women Aviators [W]
Bessie Coleman Presentation
Aviation Timeline

Denotation and Connotation * [V]

Precise Language * [G]

Selection Test [A]

© Houghton Mifflin Harcourt Publishing Company • Image Credits: (tl) ©alexandre zveiger/Shutterstock; (tr) ©YAM/Moment Select/Getty Images; (cl) ©Photo Researchers/Science History

SKILLS

- **R** Reading
- **W** Writing/Speaking & Listening/Media
- **V** Vocabulary

RESOURCES

- **G** Grammar
- **A** Assessment
- ▶ Video
- 📄 Document

* Skills covered on Unit Assessment

Collaborate & Compare

- **R** Analyze Character *
  Analyze Setting and Conflict *
- **W** Email Request
  Making of a Mentor
  20th-Century Harlem
- **V** Possessive Nouns *
- **G** Capitalization *

A

Thank You, M'am

Short Story by **Langston Hughes**

pp. 166–179 **4 Days** 660L

B

A Police Stop Changed This Teenager's Life

Article by **Amy B Wang**

pp. 180–191 **4 Days** 890L

- **R** Analyze Structure *
  Compare Characters and People *
- **W** Objective Summary
  Sketchnote the Article
  Crowdfunding
- **V** Context Clues *
- **G** More Than Enough Words *
- **A** Selection Test

A **B** pp. 192–193 **1 Day**

Reader's Choice

Find summaries and activities related to Reader's Choice texts on pp. 194–195, and find Reader's Choice texts and tests online.

from Young Arthur

Legend by **Robert D. San Souci**

830L

Perseus and the Gorgon's Head

Myth retold by **Ann Turnbull**

890L

It Couldn't Be Done

Poem by **Edgar Albert Guest**

N/A

Chemistry 101

Poem by **Marilyn Nelson**

N/A

Unit Tasks

Take Control

pp. 196–207 **5 Days**

- **W** Write an Informative Essay
- **G** Use Consistent Verb Tenses
- **W** Present a Film Critique
- **W** Reflect & Extend
  • Write a Short Story
  • Create a Vlog
- **A** Take Control Unit Test

The Terror and Wonder of Space

ESSENTIAL QUESTION:
? **Is space exploration a daring adventure or a dangerous risk?**

Analyze & Apply

Dark They Were, and Golden-Eyed
Science Fiction by Ray Bradbury

Close Read Screencast ▶

Text Sketch ENG & SPANISH 📄

Summary with Targeted Passages 📄

pp. 212–237 | **6 Days** | 540L

Analyze Science Fiction * **R**
Analyze Mood *

Literary Analysis **W**
Group Discussion
Podcast

Latin Roots * **V**

Dangling Modifiers * **G**

Selection Test **A**

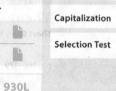

Martian Metropolis
Science Writing by Meg Thatcher

Text Sketch ENG & SPANISH 📄

Summary with Targeted Passages 📄

pp. 238–249 | **4 Days** | 930L

Analyze Central Ideas * **R**
Analyze Structure *

Fake Texts **W**
Research Becoming an Astronaut
Timeline

Greek Roots * **V**

Capitalization * **G**

Selection Test **A**

Challenges for Space Exploration
Argument by Ann Leckie

Text Sketch ENG & SPANISH 📄

Summary with Targeted Passages 📄

pp. 250–259 | **4 Days** | 880L

Analyze Author's Purpose * **R**
Analyze Repetition *

Write a Poem **W**
Chart the Risks
Examine Exploration

Word Origins * **V**

Commas After Introductory Phrases * **G**

Selection Test **A**

What If We Were Alone?
Poem by William Stafford

pp. 260–267 | **3 Days**

Analyze Form * **R**
Analyze Theme *

Write a Poem **W**
Space-Related Memes
Astronomy

Selection Test **A**

▶ Seven Minutes of Terror
Video by the National Aeronautics and Space Administration

pp. 268–271 | **3 Days** | Media

Analyze Video * **W**
Close Encounters
Make Your Own Video
Group Discussion

Selection Test **A**

SKILLS

R	Reading
W	Writing/Speaking & Listening/Media
V	Vocabulary

RESOURCES

G	Grammar
A	Assessment
	* Skills covered on Unit Assessment

▶	Video
📄	Document

Collaborate & Compare

R Analyze Argument *
Analyze Rhetorical Devices *

W Write a Letter
Explore the International Space Station
Discuss Loaded Language

V Connotations and Denotations *

G Subordinating Conjunctions in Complex Sentences *

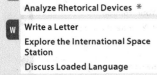

A

MENTOR TEXT

Humans Need to Explore Outer Space

Argument by **Claudia Alarcón**

Text in Focus	▶
Text Sketch ENG & SPANISH	📄
Adapted Text with Targeted Passages	📄

| pp. 272–285 | **4** Days | 1060L |

B

MENTOR TEXT

Let Robots Take to the Stars

Argument by **Eiren Caffall**

Text in Focus	▶
Text Sketch ENG & SPANISH	📄
Adapted Text with Targeted Passages	📄

| pp. 286–295 | **4** Days | 1060L |

R Compare Arguments *

W Write a Short Story
Explore Health Demands Demonstration

V Use a Dictionary *

G Subject-Verb Agreement *

A Selection Test

| A B | pp. 296–297 | **1** Day |

😊Ed

Reader's Choice

Find summaries and activities related to Reader's Choice texts on pp. 298–299, and find Reader's Choice texts and tests online.

Let's Aim for Mars **Argument** by **Buzz Aldrin** 1140L	**An Optimistic View of the World** **Personal Essay** by **Dan Tani** 970L
Your World **Poem** by **Georgia Douglas Johnson** N/A	**Sally Ride** *from* **Headstrong** **Biography** by **Rachel Swaby** 1140L

Unit Tasks

The Terror and Wonder of Space

pp. 300–311   **5** Days

W Write an Argument

G Use Transitions

W Create a Podcast

W Reflect & Extend
- Create an Infographic
- Write a Short Story

A The Terror and Wonder of Space Unit Test

Inspired by Nature

Analyze & Apply

Allied With Green
Short Story by **Naomi Shihab Nye**

Text Sketch ENG & SPANISH

Summary with Targeted Passages

pp. 316–327 | **4** Days | 880L

Analyze Theme *

Analyze Style and Figurative Language *   **R**

DM Lucy
Spill Lucy's Tea
Green Projects Brochure   **W**

Analogies *   **V**

Sentence Variety *   **G**

Selection Test   **A**

MENTOR TEXT

Never Retreat *from* Eyes Wide Open
Argument by **Paul Fleischman**

Text Sketch ENG & SPANISH

Summary with Targeted Passages

pp. 328–339 | **5** Days | 1010L

Analyze Argument *

Analyze Point of View and Purpose *   **R**

Give Your Opinion
What's Your Re-Purpose?
Energy Efficiency Infographic   **W**

Synonyms and Antonyms *   **V**

Sentence Structure *   **G**

Selection Test   **A**

from Mississippi Solo
Memoir by **Eddy Harris**

Close Read Screen Cast ▶

Text in Focus ▶

Text Sketch ENG & SPANISH

Summary with Targeted Passages

pp. 340–351 | **4** Days | 820L

Analyze Memoir *

Analyze Figurative Language *   **R**

Literary Analysis
Be Your Own BFF
Mississippi River Drawings   **W**

Figures of Speech *   **V**

Precise Language *   **G**

Selection Test   **A**

The Drought
Poem by **Amy Helfrich**

pp. 352–359 | **4** Days | N/A

Analyze Sonnet *

Analyze Rhyme Scheme *   **R**

Sonnet Experiment
Disaster Recovery
Investigate Droughts   **W**

Selection Test   **A**

SKILLS

R Reading

W Writing/Speaking & Listening/Media

V Vocabulary

RESOURCES

G Grammar

A Assessment

▶ Video

📄 Document

* Skills covered on Unit Assessment

Collaborate & Compare

R Analyze Ode *
Analyze Lyric Poetry *

W Experience in Nature
Earth Day Plan
Hold a Poetry Reading

A Selection Test

Ode to enchanted light
Poem by Pablo Neruda

Close Read Screencast ▶

Text in Focus ▶

pp. 360–369 | **3 Days** | N/A

Sleeping in the Forest
Poem by Mary Oliver

Text in Focus ▶

pp. 370–373 | **3 Days** | N/A

R Compare Forms and Elements *

W Lyric Poem
Nature's Healing Impact
Nature Web

A Selection Test

A B pp. 374–375 | **1 Day**

R Analyze Persuasive Media *
Analyze Video *

W Email NOAA
Poster Critique
Problem-Solution Chart

from Trash Talk ▶
Video by the National Oceanic and Atmospheric Administration

pp. 376–379 | **1 Day** | Media

You're Part of the Solution
Poster

pp. 380–383 | **2 Days** | N/A

R Analyze a Poster *
Compare Persuasive Media *

A Selection Test

A B pp. 384–385 | **1 Day**

Reader's Choice

Find summaries and activities related to Reader's Choice texts on pp. 386–387 and find Reader's choice texts and tests online.

from **Unbowed**
Memoir by Wangari Muta Maathai
1020L

Problems with Hurricanes
Poem by Victor Hernández Cruz
N/A

Living Large Off the Grid
Article by Kriten Mascia
920L

Haiku
Poetry by Issa, Bashō, and Busan
N/A

Unit Tasks

Inspired By Nature
pp. 388–397 | **5 Days**

W Write an Argument

G Use Commonly Confused Words Correctly

W Reflect & Extend
• Write a Research Paper
• Create a Photo Collage

A Inspired by Nature Unit Test

Game On!

ESSENTIAL QUESTION:
How do games impact our lives?

Analyze & Apply

MENTOR TEXT

Ball Hawk

Short Story by **Joseph Bruchac**

Text Sketch ENG & SPANISH

Summary with Targeted Passages

pp. 402–417 | **5** Days | 830L

Analyze Point of View * | R
Analyze Conflict * |

Epilogue | W
Baseball Card |
Player's Struggles |

Greek Roots * | V

Commonly Confused Words * | G

Selection Test | A

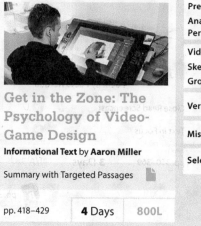

Get in the Zone: The Psychology of Video-Game Design

Informational Text by **Aaron Miller**

Summary with Targeted Passages

pp. 418–429 | **4** Days | 800L

Predict * | R
Analyze Purpose and Perspective * |

Video-Game Storyline | W
Sketchnote |
Group Discussion |

Verify Meaning * | V

Misplaced Modifiers * | G

Selection Test | A

It's Not Just a Game!

Informational Text by **Lori Calabrese**

Close Read Screencast ▶

pp. 430–441 | **5** Days | 990L

Determine Central Ideas * | R
Analyze Organizational Structure * |

Text Your Opinion | W
Sports Songs Playlist |
Present an Infographic |

Thesaurus * | V

Verbals * | G

Selection Test | A

SKILLS

R Reading

W Writing/Speaking & Listening/Media

V Vocabulary

RESOURCES

G Grammar

A Assessment

▶ Video

📄 Document

* Skills covered on Unit Assessment

Collaborate & Compare

R Analyze Novel in Verse *
Analyze Figurative Language *

W Poem with Type Effects
Podcast
Basketball Guide

 **A**

from The Crossover
Novel in Verse by **Kwame Alexander**

Text in Focus ▶

pp. 442–453 | **4** Days | N/A

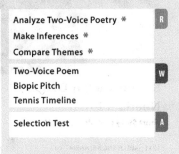 **B**

Double Doubles
Poem by **J. Patrick Lewis**

pp. 454–461 | **4** Days | N/A

Analyze Two-Voice Poetry * **R**
Make Inferences *
Compare Themes *

Two-Voice Poem **W**
Biopic Pitch
Tennis Timeline

Selection Test **A**

A B pp. 462–463 | **1** Day

Reader's Choice

Find summaries and activities related to Reader's Choice texts on pp. 464–465 and find Reader's Choice texts and tests online.

Batting After Sophie
Short Story by **Sue Macy**
760L

Amigo Brothers
Short Story by **Piri Thomas**
890L

Bridging the Generational Divide Between a Football Father and Soccer Son
Blog by **John McCormick**
1040L

Arc of Triumph
Science Writing by **Nick D'Alto**
830L

Unit Tasks

Game On!

pp. 466–475 | **5** Days

Write a Short Story **W**

Correct Punctuation of Dialogue **G**

Reflect & Extend **W**
· Write an Argument
· Create a Team Song

Game On! Unit Test **A**

Change Agents

ESSENTIAL QUESTION:
? How can changing the world change you?

Analyze & Apply

Sometimes a Dream Needs a Push
Short Story by **Walter Dean Myers**

Text Sketch ENG & SPANISH

Summary with Targeted Passages

pp. 480–493 | **4** Days | 770L

Analyze Realistic Fiction *	**R**
Analyze Character *	
Basketball Article	**W**
Dealing with Guilt	
Video Critique	
Domain-Specific Words *	**V**
Colons, Ellipses, and Hyphens *	**G**
Selection Test	**A**

Craig Kielburger Reflects on Working Toward Peace
Personal Essay by **Craig Kielburger**

Close Read Screencast

Text in Focus

Text Sketch ENG & SPANISH

Summary with Targeted Passages

pp. 494–505 | **4** Days | 1050L

Question *	**R**
Analyze Point of View and Irony *	
Mission Statement	**W**
Taking on the World	
Report on WE Charity	
Context *	**V**
Commas *	**G**
Selection Test	**A**

▶ *from* It Takes a Child
Documentary by **Judy Jackson**

pp. 506–509 | **3** Days | Media

Analyze a Documentary *	**R**
Personal Essay	**W**
Talk Comparisons	
Produce a Podcast	
Selection Test	**A**

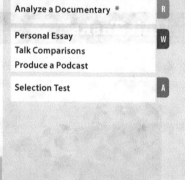

A Poem for My Librarian, Mrs. Long
Poem by **Nikki Giovanni**

pp. 510–517 | **4** Days | N/A

Analyze Themes *	**R**
Analyze Free-Verse Poetry *	
Free-Verse Poem	**W**
Ordinary Heroes	
Fake Social-Media Page	
Selection Test	**A**

SKILLS

R	Reading
W	Writing/Speaking & Listening/Media
V	Vocabulary

RESOURCES

G	Grammar
A	Assessment

▶	Video
🗎	Document

* Skills covered on Unit Assessment

Collaborate & Compare

R	Paraphrase History Writing *
	Determine Central Ideas *
W	Summary
	Primary Sources
	Advocate for Workers
V	Latin Roots *
G	Combining Sentences with Phrases *

MENTOR TEXT

Frances Perkins and the Triangle Factory Fire

History Writing by David Brooks

Text Sketch ENG & SPANISH	🗎
Summary with Targeted Passages	🗎

| pp. 518–531 | **5 Days** | 930L |

from Ashes of Roses
Novel by Mary Jane Auch

| pp. 532–547 | **6 Days** | 670L |

R	Historical Fiction *
	Setting and Motivation *
	Compare Author's Perspectives *
W	Historical Fiction
	Calm Under Pressure
	Mock Interview
V	Analogies *
G	Subject-Verb Agreement and Prepositional Phrases *
A	Selection Test

| A | B | pp. 548–549 | **1 Day** |

Reader's Choice

Find summaries and activities related to Reader's Choice texts on pp. 550–551 and find Reader's Choice texts and tests online.

from The Story of the Triangle Factory Fire
History Writing by Zachary Kent
1090L

Difference Maker: John Bergmann and Popcorn Park
Article by David Karas
1110L

from Walking with the Wind
Autobiography by John Lewis
940L

Doris is Coming
Short Story by ZZ Packer
680L

Seeing Is Believing
Informational Text by Mary Morton Cowan
1100L

Unit Tasks

Change Agents

| pp. 552–563 | **5 Days** |

W	Write a Research Report
G	Paraphrase to Avoid Plagiarism
W	Participate in a Panel Discussion
W	Reflect & Extend
	• Create a Documentary
	• Write a Short Story
A	Change Agents Unit Test

Gadgets and Glitches

ESSENTIAL QUESTION:
? **Does technology improve or control our lives?**

Analyze & Apply

The Brave Little Toaster

Science Fiction by Cory Doctorow

Text Sketch ENG & SPANISH

Summary with Targeted Passages

| pp. 4–15 | **5** Days | 990L |

Analyze Plot *   **R**
Analyze Science Fiction *

Summarize a Story   **W**
Discuss with a Small Group
Create a Comic

Context Clues *   **V**

Participles *   **G**

Selection Test   **A**

Are Bionic Superhumans on the Horizon?

Informational Text by Ramez Naam

Text Sketch ENG & SPANISH

Summary with Targeted Passages

Text in Focus ▶

| pp. 16–27 | **4** Days | 1110L |

Identify Central Ideas and Details *   **R**
Analyze Organization *

Informative Essay   **W**
Discuss with a Small Group
Create a Graphic Aid

Synonyms and Antonyms *   **V**

Commonly Confused Words *   **G**

Selection Test   **A**

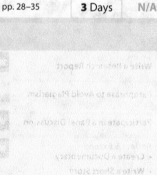

Interflora

Poem by Susan Hamlyn

| pp. 28–35 | **3** Days | N/A |

Analyze Structure *   **R**
Analyze Irony *

Sonnet   **W**
Present a Sonnet
Design a Virtual Bouquet

Selection Test   **A**

SKILLS

| R | Reading |

| W | Writing/Speaking & Listening/Media |

| V | Vocabulary |

RESOURCES

| G | Grammar |

| A | Assessment |

| ▶ | Video |

| ▤ | Document |

| * | Skills covered on Unit Assessment |

Collaborate & Compare

R	Analyze Claim and Evidence *
	Analyze Graphic Features *
W	Argue It
	Prepare for the Future
	Sketchnote
V	Use a Dictionary *
G	Transitional Words and Phrases *

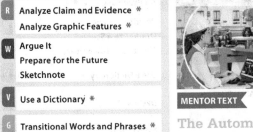

MENTOR TEXT

The Automation Paradox

Argument by **James Bessen**

Close Read Screencast ▶

pp. 36–49 | **5** Days | 1140L

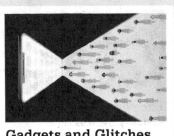

MENTOR TEXT

Heads Up, Humans

Argument by **Claudia Alarcón**

pp. 50–61 | **4** Days | 1300L

R	Evaluate Evidence *
	Analyze Rhetoric *
	Compare Arguments *
W	Create a Public Service Announcement
	Discuss with a Small Group
	My Future Job
V	Use Greek Roots *
G	Active and Passive Voice
A	Selection Test

A B | pp. 62–63 | **1** Day

Reader's Choice

Find summaries and activities related to Reader's Choice texts on pp. 64–65 and find Reader's Choice texts and tests online.

If You Go into the Woods You will Find It Has a Technology
Poem by **Heather Christle** — N/A

Hallucination
Science Fiction by **Isaac Asimov** — 790L

There Will Come Soft Rains
Science Fiction by **Ray Bradbury** — 880L

from All the Light We Cannot See
Novel by **Anthony Doerr** — 880L

Unit Tasks

Gadgets and Glitches

pp. 66–77 | **5** Days

W	Write an Argument
G	Use Transitional Words and Phrases
W	Present an Argument
W	Reflect & Extend
	• Write an Explanatory Essay
	• Create a Business Plan
A	Gadgets and Glitches Unit Test

The Thrill of Horror

Analyze & Apply

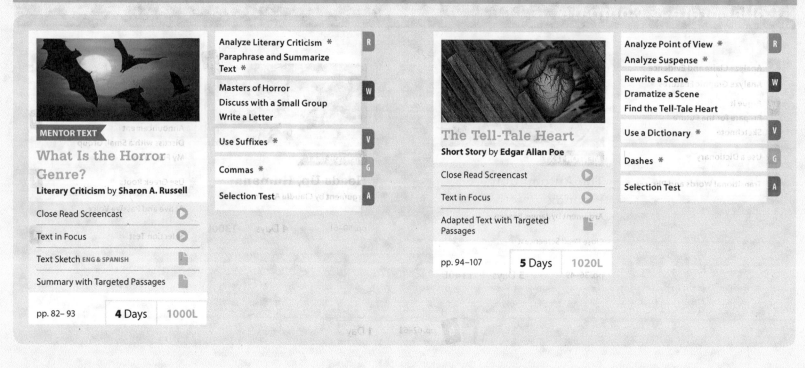

MENTOR TEXT

What Is the Horror Genre?

Literary Criticism by **Sharon A. Russell**

Close Read Screencast ▶

Text in Focus ▶

Text Sketch ENG & SPANISH 📄

Summary with Targeted Passages 📄

pp. 82–93 | **4** Days | 1000L

Analyze Literary Criticism * **R**
Paraphrase and Summarize Text *

Masters of Horror **W**
Discuss with a Small Group
Write a Letter

Use Suffixes * **V**

Commas * **G**

Selection Test **A**

The Tell-Tale Heart

Short Story by **Edgar Allan Poe**

Close Read Screencast ▶

Text in Focus ▶

Adapted Text with Targeted Passages 📄

pp. 94–107 | **5** Days | 1020L

Analyze Point of View * **R**
Analyze Suspense *

Rewrite a Scene **W**
Dramatize a Scene
Find the Tell-Tale Heart

Use a Dictionary * **V**

Dashes * **G**

Selection Test **A**

Collaborate & Compare

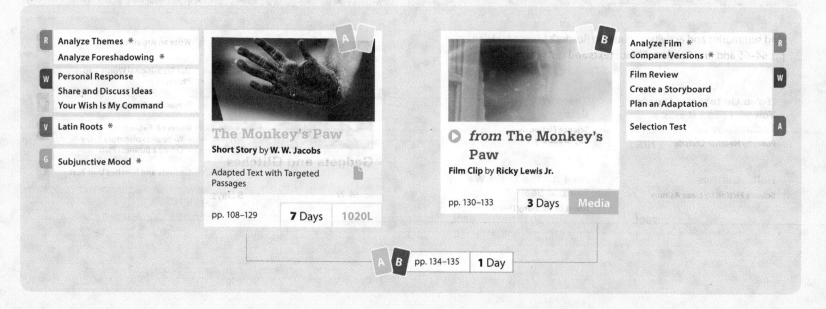

R Analyze Themes *
Analyze Foreshadowing *

W Personal Response
Share and Discuss Ideas
Your Wish Is My Command

V Latin Roots *

G Subjunctive Mood *

A

The Monkey's Paw

Short Story by **W. W. Jacobs**

Adapted Text with Targeted Passages 📄

pp. 108–129 | **7** Days | 1020L

B

▶ *from* **The Monkey's Paw**

Film Clip by **Ricky Lewis Jr.**

pp. 130–133 | **3** Days | Media

Analyze Film * **R**
Compare Versions *

Film Review **W**
Create a Storyboard
Plan an Adaptation

Selection Test **A**

A B pp. 134–135 | **1** Day

⦾ Ed

SKILLS

R	Reading
W	Writing/Speaking & Listening/Media
V	Vocabulary

RESOURCES

G	Grammar
A	Assessment
▶	Video
📄	Document

* Skills covered on Unit Assessment

Collaborate & Compare

R
Analyze Epic Poetry *
Analyze an Adaptation *

W
Video-Game Storyline
Create a Character Profile
Create a Virtual Tour

A

from The Aeneid of Virgil

Epic Poem translated by **Allen Mandelbaum**

| pp. 136–142 | **2** Days | N/A |

B

from Hades: Lord of the Dead

Graphic Novel by **George O'Connor**

| pp. 143–155 | **4** Days | N/A |

R Compare Versions *

A Selection Test

A B | pp. 156–157 | **1** Day |

Reader's Choice

⦾ Ed

Find summaries and activities related to Reader's Choice texts on pp. 158–159, and find Reader's Choice texts and tests online.

Frankenstein
Poem by **Edward Field**
| | N/A |

beware: do not read this poem
Poem by **Ishmael Reed**
| | N/A |

Blood
Short Story by **Zdravka Evitmova**
| | 660L |

The Outsider
Short Story by **H. P. Lovecraft**
| | 1220L |

Scary Tales
Essay by **Jackie Torrence**
| | 580L |

Unit Tasks

The Thrill of Horror

| pp. 160–169 | **5** Days |

W Write a Literary Analysis

G Use Commas

W Reflect & Extend
• Write a Short Story
• Create a Movie Trailer

A The Thrill of Horror Unit Test

Places We Call Home

ESSENTIAL QUESTION:
? *What are the places that shape who you are?*

Analyze & Apply

MENTOR TEXT

from **The Book of the Unknown Americans**
Novel by Cristina Henríquez

Text Sketch ENG & SPANISH

Summary with Targeted Passages

| pp. 174–189 | **6** Days | 870L |

Analyze Plot * — R
Analyze Themes *

Get Inside a Character's Head — W
Create a Collage
Perform a Scene

Use a Dictionary * — V

Ellipses * — G

Selection Test — A

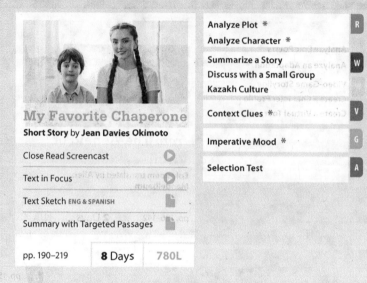

My Favorite Chaperone

Short Story by Jean Davies Okimoto

Close Read Screencast ▶

Text in Focus

Text Sketch ENG & SPANISH

Summary with Targeted Passages

| pp. 190–219 | **8** Days | 780L |

Analyze Plot * — R
Analyze Character *

Summarize a Story — W
Discuss with a Small Group
Kazakh Culture

Context Clues * — V

Imperative Mood * — G

Selection Test — A

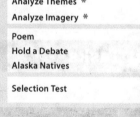

Spirit Walking in the Tundra

Poem by Joy Harjo

| pp. 220–227 | **4** Days | N/A |

Analyze Themes * — R
Analyze Imagery *

Poem — W
Hold a Debate
Alaska Natives

Selection Test — A

SKILLS

- **R** Reading
- **W** Writing/Speaking & Listening/Media
- **V** Vocabulary

RESOURCES

- **G** Grammar
- **A** Assessment
- ▶ Video
- 📄 Document

* Skills covered on Unit Assessment

Collaborate & Compare

- **W** Evaluate a Documentary *
  Write a Letter
  Discuss with a Small Group
  Create an Infographic
- **V** Multiple-Meaning Words *
- **G** Semicolons, Colons, and Parentheses *

A

▶ **New Immigrants Share Their Stories**
Documentary produced by **The Working Group**

pp. 228–230 | **1** Day | Media

B

A Common Bond
Informational Text by **Brooke Hauser**

pp. 231–245 | **5** Days | 1150L

- **R** Analyze Text Elements *
  Compare Purposes *
- **A** Selection Test

A **B** pp. 246–247 | **1** Day

Reader's Choice

Find summaries and activities related to Reader's Choice texts on pp. 248–249 and find Reader's choice texts and tests online.

My Father and the Figtree
Poem by **Naomi Shihab Nye**
N/A

Golden Glass
Short Story by **Alma Luz Villanueva**
930L

A Place to Call Home
Research Study by **Scott Bittle** and **Jonathan Rochkind**
1160L

Salmon Boy
Myth by **Michael J. Caduto** and **Joseph Bruchac**
700L

Unit Tasks

Places We Call Home

pp. 250–259 | **5** Days

- **W** Write a Short Story
- **G** Use Dashes and Ellipses
- **W** Reflect & Extend
  • Write an Article
  • Create a Photo Collection
- **A** Places We Call Home Unit Test

The Fight for Freedom

ESSENTIAL QUESTION:
What will people risk to be free?

Analyze & Apply

from Narrative of the Life of Frederick Douglass, an American Slave
Autobiography by Frederick Douglass

Close Read Screencast ▶

Text in Focus ▶

Text Sketch ENG & SPANISH

Adapted Text with Targeted Passages

pp. 264–275   **5** Days   1070L

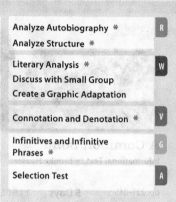

Analyze Autobiography *   R
Analyze Structure *

Literary Analysis *   W
Discuss with Small Group
Create a Graphic Adaptation

Connotation and Denotation *   V

Infinitives and Infinitive Phrases *   G

Selection Test   A

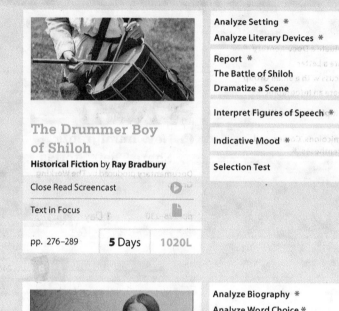

The Drummer Boy of Shiloh
Historical Fiction by Ray Bradbury

Close Read Screencast ▶

Text in Focus

pp. 276–289   **5** Days   1020L

Analyze Setting *   R
Analyze Literary Devices *

Report *   W
The Battle of Shiloh
Dramatize a Scene

Interpret Figures of Speech *   V

Indicative Mood *   G

Selection Test   A

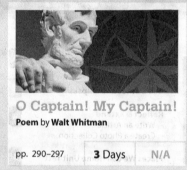

O Captain! My Captain!
Poem by Walt Whitman

pp. 290–297   **3** Days   N/A

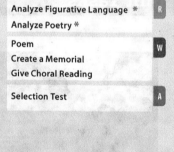

Analyze Figurative Language *   R
Analyze Poetry *

Poem   W
Create a Memorial
Give Choral Reading

Selection Test   A

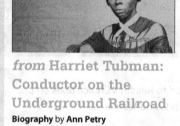

from Harriet Tubman: Conductor on the Underground Railroad
Biography by Ann Petry

pp. 298–317   **6** Days   1020L

Analyze Biography *   R
Analyze Word Choice *

Speech *   W
Create a Timeline
Tubman and Douglass

Use Latin Roots *   V

Conditional Mood *   G

Selection Test   A

SKILLS

R	Reading
W	Writing/Speaking & Listening/Media
V	Vocabulary

RESOURCES

G	Grammar
A	Assessment
▶	Video
📄	Document

* Skills covered on Unit Assessment

Collaborate & Compare

R	Analyze Figurative Language *
	Analyze Chronological Order *
W	Letter
	Express Ideas Visually
	Recite a Poem

Not My Bones
Poem by Marilyn Nelson

pp. 318–325 | **2** Days | N/A

MENTOR TEXT

from Fortune's Bones
History Writing by Pamela Espeland

Summary with Targeted Passages 📄

Text Sketch ENG & SPANISH 📄

pp. 326–331 | **3** Days | 790L

| R | Compare Treatments * |
| A | Selection Test |

A B | pp. 332–333 | **1** Day

Reader's Choice

🙂 Ed

Find summaries and activities related to Reader's Choice texts on pp. 334–335 and find Reader's Choice texts and tests online.

I Saw Old General at Bay
Poem by Walt Whitman

N/A

A Mystery of Heroism
Short Story by Stephan Crane

990L

from Bloody Times: The Funeral of Abraham Lincoln and the Manhunt for Jefferson Davis
History Writing by James L. Swanson

Civil War Journal
Journal by Louisa May Alcott

1370L

My Friend Douglass
Biography by Russel Freedman

1220L

Unit Tasks

The Fight for Freedom

pp. 336–347 | **5** Days

W	Write a Research Report
G	Use Verb Moods
W	Participate in a Collaborative Discussion
W	Reflect & Extend
	• Write a Short Story
	• Create an Infographic
A	The Fight for Freedom Unit Test

Finding Your Path

? **ESSENTIAL QUESTION:**
How do the challenges you face today help to shape your future?

Analyze & Apply

from **Bronx Masquerade**
Novel by Nikki Grimes

Close Read Screencast ▶

Text Sketch ENG & SPANISH 📄

Summary with Targeted Passages 📄

pp. 352–365 | **5** Days | 710L

Analyze Perspectives * **R**
Analyze Characterization *

Write a Poem **W**
Present a Poem
Discuss as a Small Group

Use Context Clues * **V**

Gerunds * **G**

Selection Test **A**

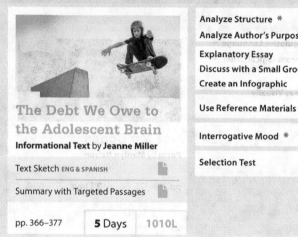

The Debt We Owe to the Adolescent Brain
Informational Text by Jeanne Miller

Text Sketch ENG & SPANISH 📄

Summary with Targeted Passages 📄

pp. 366–377 | **5** Days | 1010L

Analyze Structure * **R**
Analyze Author's Purpose *

Explanatory Essay **W**
Discuss with a Small Group
Create an Infographic

Use Reference Materials * **V**

Interrogative Mood * **G**

Selection Test **A**

Collaborate & Compare

R Compare Poetic Structure *

W Literary Analysis
Give a Dramatic Reading
Discuss with a Small Group

A

Hanging Fire
Poem by Audre Lorde

pp. 378–384 | **2** Days | N/A

B

Summer of His Fourteenth Year
Poem by Gloria Amescua

pp. 385–389 | **3** Days | N/A

Compare Poems * **R**

Selection Test **A**

A B pp. 390–391 | **1** Day

⌣Ed

SKILLS

R Reading

W Writing/Speaking & Listening/Media

V Vocabulary

RESOURCES

G Grammar

A Assessment

▶ Video

📄 Document

* Skills covered on Unit Assessment

Collaborate & Compare

R Analyze Claim and Evidence *
Identify Counterclaims *

W Opinion Piece
Media Messages
Social Media

V Context Clues *

G Shifts in Voice and Mood *

A

MENTOR TEXT

It's Complicated: The Social Lives of Networked Teens

Argument by danah boyd

Text in Focus	▶
Text Sketch ENG & SPANISH	📄
Summary with Targeted Passages	📄

| pp. 392–403 | **4** Days | 1080L |

B

Outsmart Your Smartphone

Argument by Catherine Steiner-Adair

| Text in Focus | ▶ |

| pp. 404–417 | **6** Days | 1110L |

R Analyze Structure *
Analyze Rhetorical Devices *
Compare Arguments *

W Email
Critique as a Class
Technology Topics

V Word Families *

G Parallel Structure *

A Selection Test

| A B | pp. 418–419 | **1** Day |

⌣Ed

Reader's Choice

Find summaries and activities related to Reader's Choice texts on pp. 420–421 and find Reader's Choice texts and tests online.

Teenagers
Poem by Pat Mora

N/A

Identity
Poem by Julio Noboa Polanco

N/A

Hard on the Gas
Poem by Janet S. Wong

N/A

Marigolds
Short Story by Eugenia Collier

1020L

My Summer of Scooping Ice Cream
Essay by Shonda Rhimes

810L

Unit Tasks

Finding Your Path

pp. 422–433   **5** Days

W Write an Argument

G Use Gerunds Correctly

W Present an Argument

W Reflect & Extend
· Personal Narrative
· Envision Your Future Self

A **Finding Your Path** Unit Test

The Legacy of Anne Frank

Analyze & Apply

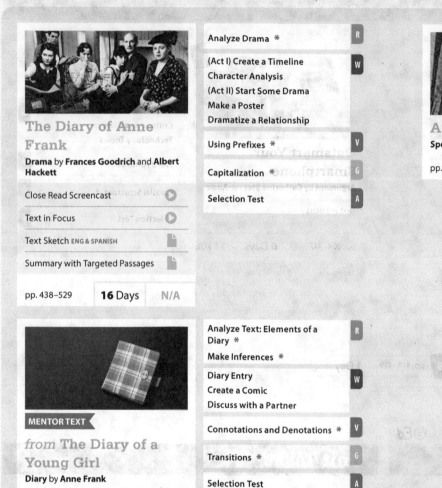

The Diary of Anne Frank

Drama by Frances Goodrich and Albert Hackett

Close Read Screencast ▶

Text in Focus ▶

Text Sketch ENG & SPANISH 📄

Summary with Targeted Passages 📄

pp. 438–529 | **16** Days | N/A

| Analyze Drama * | R |

(Act I) Create a Timeline
Character Analysis
(Act II) Start Some Drama
Make a Poster
Dramatize a Relationship | W |

Using Prefixes * | V |

Capitalization * | G |

Selection Test | A |

MENTOR TEXT

from The Diary of a Young Girl

Diary by Anne Frank

Text Sketch ENG & SPANISH 📄

Summary with Targeted Passages 📄

pp. 530–541 | **4** Days | 990L

| Analyze Text: Elements of a Diary *
Make Inferences * | R |

Diary Entry
Create a Comic
Discuss with a Partner | W |

Connotations and Denotations * | V |

Transitions * | G |

Selection Test | A |

After Auschwitz

Speech by Elie Wiesel

pp. 542–551 | **4** Days | 920L

| Analyze Appeals *
Analyze Rhetorical Devices * | R |

Speech
Make a Poster
Discuss with a Group | W |

Selection Test | A |

SKILLS
- **R** Reading
- **W** Writing/Speaking & Listening/Media
- **V** Vocabulary
- * Skills covered on Unit Assessment

RESOURCES
- **G** Grammar
- **A** Assessment
- ▶ Video
- 📄 Document

Ⓔ Ed

Collaborate & Compare

R Analyze Sound Devices *
Analyze Figurative Language *
W Literary Analysis
Recite a Poem
Pick a Poet

A
There But for the Grace
Poem by **Wisława Szymborska**
pp. 552–557 | **3 Days** | N/A

B
Days
Poem by **Billy Collins**
pp. 558–561 | **3 Days** | N/A

Compare Poems * **R**
Selection Test **A**

A B pp. 562–563 | **1 Day**

Ⓔ Ed

Reader's Choice

Find summaries and activities related to Reader's Choice texts on pp. 564–565 and find Reader's Choice texts and tests online.

Peace Can Happen
Essay by **Christine Kingery**
720L

The Butterfly / On a Sunny Evening
Poem by **Pavel Friedmann / Anonymous**
N/A

The Singing Women
Short Story by **Rebecca Makkai**
970L

from **A Tragedy Revealed: A Heroine's Last Days**
Article by **Ernst Schnabel**
990L

Nobel Prize Acceptance Speech
Speech by **Elie Wiesel**
790L

Unit Tasks

The Legacy of Anne Frank
pp. 566–575 | **5 Days**

Write a Personal Narrative **W**
Use Correct Capitalization **G**
Reflect & Extend **W**
- Write a Persuasive Essay
- Create a Theme Song
The Legacy of Anne Frank Unit Test **A**

Acknowledgments

Cover Illustration from *A Chance in the World* by Steve Pemberton. Copyright © 2012 by Thomas Nelson. Reprinted by permission of Thomas Nelson.

Cover Illustration from *The Crossover* by Kwame Alexander. Illustration copyright © 2014 by Houghton Mifflin Harcourt Publishing Company. Reprinted by permission of Houghton Mifflin Harcourt Publishing Company.

Cover Illustration from *Life As We Knew It* by Susan Beth Pfeffer. Illustration copyright © 2008 by Houghton Mifflin Harcourt Publishing Company. Reprinted by permission of Houghton Mifflin Harcourt Publishing Company.

"Mirror Image" by Lena Coakley. Text copyright © 1998 by Lena Coakley. Reprinted by permission of the author.

Excerpt from *Monster* by Walter Dean Myers. Text copyright © 1999 by Walter Dean Myers. Reprinted by permission of HarperCollins Publishers.

Excerpt from *Monster: A Graphic Novel* by Walter Dean Myers, adapted by Guy A Sims, illustrated by Dawud Anyabwile. Text copyright © 1999 by Walter Dean Myers and © 2015 by the Estate of Walter Dean Myers. Illustrations copyright © 2015. Reprinted by permissions of HarperCollins Publishers.

Cover Illustration from *Path to the Stars: My Journey from Girl Scout to Rocket Scientist* by Sylvia Acevedo. Illustration copyright © 2020 by Houghton Mifflin Harcourt Publishing Company. Reprinted by permission of Houghton Mifflin Harcourt Publishing Company.

Cover Illustration from *Peak* by Roland Smith. Illustration copyright © 2008 by Houghton Mifflin Harcourt Publishing Company. Reprinted by permission of Houghton Mifflin Harcourt Publishing Company.

Cover Illustration from *Reaching Out* by Francisco Jiménez. Illustration copyright © 2009 by Houghton Mifflin Harcourt Publishing Company. Reprinted by permission of Houghton Mifflin Harcourt Publishing Company.

Excerpts from "Thank you M'am" from *Short Stories* by Langston Hughes. Text copyright © 1996 by Ramona Bass and Arnold Rampersad. Reprinted by permission of Hill and Wang, a division of Farrar, Straus & Giroux, Inc. and Harold Ober Associates. CAUTION: Users are warned that this work is protected under copyright laws and downloading is strictly prohibited. The right to reproduce or transfer the work via any medium must be secured with Farrar, Straus and Giroux.

Image Credits

62 (bl) looking up ©Carrie Garcia/HMH, skyline ©andersphoto/Shutterstock; (bc) ©Jean Marc-Giboux/HMH; 66 (t) ©Lester Laminack; (b) ©Heinemann; (t to b) ©Maximova Evgeniya/Shutterstock; letter T ©Yaten Tau/Shutterstock, question mark ©Roman Sigaev/Shutterstock; ©teploleta/Adobe Stock; symbols ©teploleta/Adobe Stock, speech bubbles ©art_of_sun/Adobe Stock; ©Ginger Lemon/Adobe Stock; ©TonTonic/Shutterstock; ©art_of_sun/Adobe Stock; ©Maximova Evgeniya/Shutterstock; ©Annaartist/Shutterstock; letter W ©Yaten Tau/Shutterstock, arrows ©Maximova Evgeniya/Shutterstock; 120 ©Abigail Bobo/HMH; 126 (l) 7 Minutes of Terror: ©NASA Jet Propulsion Laboratory